AAT

Personal Tax FA 2016

AQ 2013 Level 4

Course Book

For assessments from
1 January 2017

Second edition December 2016
ISBN 9781 5097 1076 8
ISBN (for internal use only) 9781 5097 1083 6

British Library Cataloguing-in-Publication Data
A catalogue record for this book is available from the British Library

Published by

BPP Learning Media Ltd
BPP House, Aldine Place
142-144 Uxbridge Road
London W12 8AA

www.bpp.com/learningmedia

Printed in the United Kingdom by RICOH UK Limited
Unit 2
Wells Place
Merstham
RH1 3LG

Contents

Introduction to the course

Syllabus overview

The general purpose of this unit is to enable learners to understand the impact and significance of taxation on individuals. All sources of income for individuals, such as employment income, capital gains, income from land and property and investment income are covered. By studying these taxes, learners can appreciate the tax implications for their own personal situation, and that of clients.

Test specification for this unit assessment

Assessment type	Marking type	Duration of exam
Computer based unit assessment	Computer and human marked	2 hours

Learning outcomes	
1	Understand legislation and procedures relating to personal tax
2	Calculate income from all sources and identify taxable and non-taxable items
3	Apply current legislation to calculate the tax payable on income
4	Account for capital gains tax according to current legislation
5	Prepare accurate computations and complete relevant parts of the self-assessment tax returns

Assessment structure

2 hours duration

Competency is 70%

*Note that this is only a guideline as to what might come up. The format and content of each task may vary from what we have listed below.

Your exam will consist of 11 tasks.

Task	Expected content	Max marks	Chapter ref	Study complete
Task 1	**Benefits in kind** Provision of cars (including fuel for private motoring and pool cars)	9	Employment income	
Task 2	**Benefits in kind** All excluding cars including: • Beneficial loans • Living accommodation including job related accommodation • Use of assets • Pool cars • Vans, including fuel for private motoring • Other taxable and non-taxable benefits Note. Employment income is a key task and will feature in multiple tasks within the assessment. Students can expect questions on: • The difference between, and indicators of, employment and self-employment • The basis of assessment for employment income • Income assessable from employment income	10	Employment income	

Task	Expected content	Max marks	Chapter ref	Study complete
Task 3	**Income from property** Students can expect questions on: • Furnished and unfurnished property • Rent a room schemes • Furnished holiday lettings • Buy-to-let investments	10	Property income	
Task 4	**Investment income** Students can expect questions on: • Bank interest • Building society interest • Dividends • Individual savings accounts	6	Taxable income	
Task 5	**Computation of total and taxable income** This could include: • The implication of paying a pension/making a charitable gift • Implication of personal allowances	12	Taxable income	
Task 6	**Computation and payment of tax** Assessed via free text box. Human marked. Students will need to be able to • Collate different types of income subject to income tax and • Apply the rules for different tax bands and rates. • This includes all rates for all levels and types of income. The impact of charity giving and pensions will need to be understood. An understanding of the payments on account system is crucial.	10	Calculation of income tax Payment of tax and tax administration	

Task	Expected content	Max marks	Chapter ref	Study complete
Task 7	**Theory underpinning topic and penalties** Assessed via free text box. Human marked. The questions will usually be client focussed so students will be expected to address their answers in an appropriate manner. Students can expect written questions on: • What taxation documentation individuals need to maintain and for how long • The responsibilities individuals have for disclosing full and accurate information to HMRC • The duties and responsibilities tax practitioners have to clients and HMRC • The sources of tax information for individuals • How the various penalties and interest are applied by HMRC in relation to filing and payment processes for income tax and capital gains tax.	10	All	
Task 8	**Tax returns** There are three tax returns which are assessable: • Employment income • Property income • Capital gains These are expected to be completed with accuracy and completed in conjunction with the student's own figures, if appropriate. This task is human marked.	7	Employment income Property income Chargeable gains	

Task	Expected content	Max marks	Chapter ref	Study complete
Task 9	**Basics of capital gains tax** Computations can be expected on: • Chargeable assets being disposed of • Enhancement expenditure • Part disposals • Chattels • Connected parties	12	Chargeable gains	
Task 10	**Taxation of shares** Computations will include matching rules, bonus issues and rights issues. Assessed by free text box and human marked.	8	Share disposals	
Task 11	**Capital gains tax exemptions, losses, reliefs and tax payable** Exempt assets include principal private residence. Students need to be able to • Apply the annual exempt amount • Understand how the relief for losses work. • Compute the actual capital gains tax payable, based on the individual's income tax situation	6	Chargeable gains Principal private residence	

Skills bank

Our experience of preparing students for this type of assessment suggests that to obtain competency, you will need to develop a number of key skills.

What do I need to know to do well in the assessment?

This unit is one of the optional Level 4 units. To be successful in the assessment you need to be able to:

- Calculate employment income including benefits in kind

- Calculate property income

- Produce a schedule showing income from all sources including investment income

- Calculate the personal allowance a taxpayer is entitled to

- Calculate income tax for a wide range of taxpayers including those who have given money to charity or paid into a pension

- Explain key elements of the syllabus in writing including the rules for payment of tax and submission of tax returns

- Complete a page from a tax return

- Calculate the chargeable gains arising in different scenarios including the disposal of shares and private residences.

Assumed knowledge

No prior knowledge of tax is expected but if you have worked in tax or previously studied the *Business Tax* unit then you will have an immediate advantage.

Assessment style

In the assessment you will complete tasks by:

1   Entering narrative by selecting from drop down menus of narrative options known as **picklists**

2   Using **drag and drop** menus to enter narrative

3   Typing in numbers, known as **gapfill** entry

4   Entering **ticks**

5   Entering **dates** by selecting from a calendar

6   Writing written explanations in a very basic word processing environment which has limited editing and no spelling or grammar checking functionality

7   Entering detailed calculations in a very basic spreadsheet environment that has limited editing functionality and will not perform calculations for you

You must familiarise yourself with the style of the online questions and the AAT software before taking the assessment. As part of your revision, login to the **AAT**

website and attempt their **online practice assessments. Do check that the assessments have been updated to Finance Act 2016.**

Introduction to the assessment

The question practice you do will prepare you for the format of tasks you will see in the *Personal Taxation* assessment. It is also useful to familiarise yourself with the introductory information you **may** be given at the start of the assessment.

1   As you revise, use the **BPP Passcards** to consolidate your knowledge. They are a pocket-sized revision tool, perfect for packing in that last-minute revision.

2   Attempt as many tasks as possible in the **Question Bank**. There are plenty of assessment-style tasks which are excellent preparation for the real assessment.

3   Always **check** through your own answers as you will in the real assessment, before looking at the solutions in the back of the Question Bank.

Key to icons

 Key term
A key definition which is important to be aware of for the assessment

 Formula to learn
A formula you will need to learn as it will not be provided in the assessment

 Formula provided
A formula which is provided within the assessment and generally available as a pop-up on screen

 Activity
An example which allows you to apply your knowledge to the technique covered in the Course Book. The solution is provided at the end of the chapter

 Illustration
A worked example which can be used to review and see how an assessment question could be answered

 Assessment focus point
A high priority point for the assessment

 Open book reference
Where use of an open book will be allowed for the assessment

 Real life examples
A practical real life scenario

Supplements

From time to time we may need to publish supplementary materials to one of our titles. This can be for a variety of reasons, from a small change in the AAT unit guidance to new legislation coming into effect between editions.

You should check our supplements page regularly for anything that may affect your learning materials. All supplements are available free of charge on our supplements page on our website at:

www.bpp.com/learning-media/about/students

Improving material and removing errors

There is a constant need to update and enhance our study materials in line with both regulatory changes and new insights into the assessments.

From our team of authors BPP appoints a subject expert to update and improve these materials for each new edition.

Their updated draft is subsequently technically checked by another author and from time to time non-technically checked by a proof reader.

We are very keen to remove as many numerical errors and narrative typos as we can but given the volume of detailed information being changed in a short space of time we know that a few errors will sometimes get through our net.

We apologise in advance for any inconvenience that an error might cause. We continue to look for new ways to improve these study materials and would welcome your suggestions. Please feel free to contact our AAT Head of Programme at nisarahmed@bpp.com if you have any suggestions for us.

The tax framework

Learning outcomes

1.1K	Explain the main current legislation relating to personal taxation
1.3K	Explain the responsibilities that individuals have for disclosure of income and payment of tax to the relevant tax authorities
1.5K	Describe the duties and responsibilities of a tax practitioner
5.1S	Make computations and submissions in accordance with current tax law

Assessment context

This chapter provides you with important background to your syllabus. The issues discussed in this chapter could be tested as part of the 10 marks available for Task 7.

Qualification context

Professional ethics are vital for a member of the AAT. The tax knowledge in this chapter is useful background in the *Business Tax* course.

Business context

A tax practitioner needs to know the duties and obligations that they owe to their client, the tax authorities and the Government.

A tax practitioner needs to know and understand the detailed tax rules.

Chapter overview

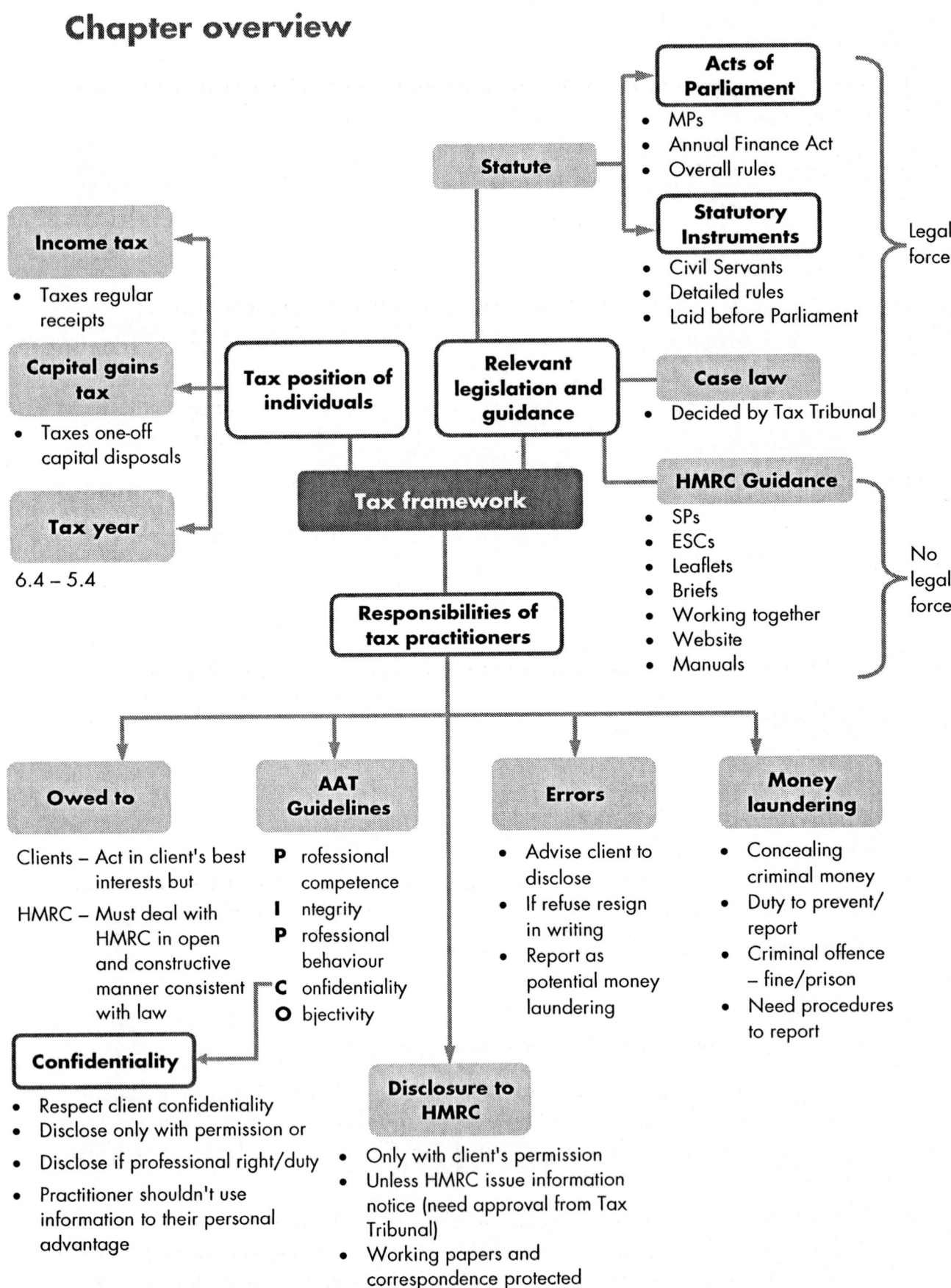

Acts of Parliament
- MPs
- Annual Finance Act
- Overall rules

Statutory Instruments
- Civil Servants
- Detailed rules
- Laid before Parliament

Legal force

Statute

Income tax
- Taxes regular receipts

Capital gains tax
- Taxes one-off capital disposals

Tax year

6.4 – 5.4

Tax position of individuals

Relevant legislation and guidance

Case law
- Decided by Tax Tribunal

Tax framework

HMRC Guidance
- SPs
- ESCs
- Leaflets
- Briefs
- Working together
- Website
- Manuals

No legal force

Responsibilities of tax practitioners

Owed to
- Clients – Act in client's best interests but
- HMRC – Must deal with HMRC in open and constructive manner consistent with law

Confidentiality
- Respect client confidentiality
- Disclose only with permission or
- Disclose if professional right/duty
- Practitioner shouldn't use information to their personal advantage

AAT Guidelines

P rofessional competence
I ntegrity
P rofessional behaviour
C onfidentiality
O bjectivity

Disclosure to HMRC
- Only with client's permission
- Unless HMRC issue information notice (need approval from Tax Tribunal)
- Working papers and correspondence protected

Errors
- Advise client to disclose
- If refuse resign in writing
- Report as potential money laundering

Money laundering
- Concealing criminal money
- Duty to prevent/report
- Criminal offence – fine/prison
- Need procedures to report

BPP
LEARNING MEDIA

Introduction

This chapter introduces you to some key background principles which will underlie all of your taxation studies.

1 Tax position of individuals

1.1 Liability to tax

Individuals pay the following taxes:

Key term

Income tax	This is paid on income (receipts which are expected to recur, for example the monthly receipt of a salary or rent received from an investment property).
Capital gains tax	This is paid on capital gains (one-off profits on disposal of capital items, for example the sale of an investment property).

1.2 Her Majesty's Revenue & Customs

Income tax and capital gains tax are administered by **Her Majesty's Revenue & Customs (HMRC)**.

1.3 Tax year

Key term

The tax year	This runs from 6 April to the following 5 April. It is also known as the **fiscal year** or the **year of assessment**. Tax is calculated on the income earned and gains realised in the tax year.

The year of assessment 2016/17 runs from 6 April 2016 to 5 April 2017.

Some taxpayers will have to complete a tax return and pay tax under the self-assessment system. However, most taxpayers will have all their tax deducted at source. There is therefore no requirement for these taxpayers to complete a return.

2 Relevant law and guidance from HMRC

2.1 Legislation

The Government creates tax law. Tax laws consist of:

- **Acts of Parliament** – These are created via MPs debating in Parliament. There are a number of Acts that give the main rules for each of the UK taxes. These are updated each year by the annual **Finance Act**. Periodically they will be rewritten from scratch.

- **Statutory Instruments (SI)** – These are created by civil servants acting on behalf of the **Chancellor of the Exchequer**. They include the detailed rules for the operation of UK taxes. An SI will be laid before Parliament and becomes law if no objections are raised.

2.2 Case law

A taxpayer and HMRC may disagree over the interpretation of the **legislation**. Such disagreements will be heard by the **Tax Tribunal**. Once a decision has been reached, this has the force of law so all future taxpayers and HMRC officers must follow the decision.

2.3 HMRC guidance

HMRC publishes a range of guidance material to advise taxpayers as to how it interprets the law. These include:

Guidance document	What it does
Statements of practice	These set out how HMRC intends to apply the law.
Extra statutory concessions	These set out the circumstances when HMRC will not apply the letter of law because they believe it would be unfair to do so.
Explanatory leaflets	These explain key rules in simple terms.
Revenue and Customs briefs	These give HMRC's view on specific issues.
Internal guidance	These are manuals used by HMRC staff.
Working together	This is guidance for tax practitioners.

For information see www.gov.uk/government/organisations/hm-revenue-customs (please note all information required for the exam is included in this Course Book).

HMRC guidance does not have legal force.

3 Responsibilities of tax practitioners

3.1 Responsibility to clients and HMRC

A tax practitioner should act in the best interests of their client.

However, they must deal with HMRC staff in an open and constructive manner consistent with the law.

3.2 AAT guidelines on professional ethics

There are five fundamental principles which AAT members must follow:

Fundamental principle	What it means
Professional competence and due care	A member must keep up to date technically and act diligently in accordance with current practice.
Integrity	A member must be straightforward and honest.
Professional behaviour	A member must comply with relevant laws and regulations and must not bring the profession into disrepute.
Confidentiality	See below.
Objectivity	A member must make decisions free from bias and not be influenced by other parties or his/her own interests.

(AAT, 2014)

3.3 Confidentiality

A member must respect a client's confidentiality.

Information may only be disclosed to third parties if the client has authorised this.

A member may disclose information to the authorities if there is a professional right or obligation to disclose (for example **money laundering**).

A member should not use confidential client information for their own advantage.

3.4 Disclosure to HMRC

Usually, a practitioner would only disclose information to HMRC with the taxpayer's permission.

If the taxpayer does not co-operate with HMRC, then HMRC may issue a written 'information notice'. This must be approved by the Tax Tribunal. The notice would force the practitioner to provide HMRC with requested information or documents.

HMRC may not obtain the practitioner's working papers or correspondence between the practitioner and the taxpayer.

3.5 Material error or omission

If a member learns of an error, omission or a failure to file a tax return, the member should bring this to the taxpayer's attention and request permission to disclose this to HMRC.

If the taxpayer refuses to disclose, then the member should notify the taxpayer in writing that they are unable to continue to act for them.

Members in practice must report this to their Money Laundering Reporting Officer or, if the member is a sole practitioner, the National Crime Agency (NCA). The taxpayer should not be advised that a report has been made.

3.6 Money laundering

Money laundering is the process by which the origins of criminal money are concealed.

AAT members must act to prevent money laundering and to report suspicions of it to the authorities.

Failure to prevent or report is a criminal offence leading to a fine and/or imprisonment.

A member's suspicions should be reported to their firm's money laundering officer. A sole practitioner should report to the authorities directly.

Chapter summary

- Individuals may have to pay income tax and/or capital gains tax.
- HMRC is responsible for the administration of tax.
- The tax year runs from 6 April in one year to the following 5 April.
- Some of the rules governing tax are laid down in statute law, while some are laid down in case law.
- HMRC provides guidance about how tax law works, for example in Statements of practice, Extra statutory concessions and Revenue & Customs briefs.
- Tax practitioners have responsibilities to their clients and to HMRC.
- The ethical guideline of confidentiality means that a client's tax affairs should not be discussed with third parties without the client's permission, unless there is a legal right or obligation for the adviser to disclose the information.
- Tax practitioners may be required to produce information to HMRC.
- A tax practitioner must cease to act for a client who refuses to disclose an error or omission to HMRC, and must make a money laundering report.
- Money laundering occurs when the proceeds of criminal activities are converted into assets which appear to have a non-criminal origin.

Keywords

- **Acts of Parliament:** laws produced by MPs debating in Parliament

- **Capital gains tax:** tax charged on the profits made on the disposal of capital items

- **Case law:** decisions of the Tax Tribunal about the interpretation of tax statutes which serve as a further source of tax law

- **Her Majesty's Revenue & Customs (HMRC):** responsible for the administration of tax

- **Income tax:** tax charged on money a taxpayer regularly receives

- **Legislation:** laws created by the Government. These include Acts of Parliament and Statutory Instruments

- **Money laundering:** proceeds of criminal activities converted into assets which appear to have a non-criminal origin

- **Statutory instrument:** laws produced by civil servants acting on behalf of the Chancellor of the Exchequer

- **The tax year (fiscal year or year of assessment):** the 12-month period that runs from 6 April in one year to 5 April in the next year. Thus the tax year 2016/17 runs from 6 April 2016 to 5 April 2017

Test your learning

1   **Identify whether the statement below is true or false.**

Statement	True ✓	False ✓
All taxpayers are sent a tax return each year by HM Revenue & Customs.		✓

2   **The tax administration within the UK is undertaken by:**

   Tick ONE box.

	✓
The Chancellor of the Exchequer	
Companies House	
HM Revenue & Customs	✓
Members of Parliament	

3   **Indicate with ticks which TWO of the following have the force of law.**

	✓
Acts of Parliament	✓
HMRC Statements of practice	
Statutory Instruments	✓
Extra statutory concessions	

4   **When is a tax practitioner not bound by the ethical Guidelines of client confidentiality?**

   Tick ONE box.

	✓
When in a social environment	
When discussing client affairs with third parties with the client's proper and specific authority	✓
When reading documents relating to a client's affairs in public places	
When preparing tax returns	✓

5   **Who should a sole practitioner make a report to if they suspect a client of money laundering?**

Tick ONE box.

	✓
HMRC	
Nearest police station	
National Crime Agency	✓
Tax Tribunal	

6   Cornelius is an acquaintance of your client, Ruby, as they have similar jobs in similar sized companies. He knows that Ruby was made redundant recently. He is facing redundancy himself and would like to know how much redundancy money Ruby received so that he can compare this to the figure his company is offering him.

State how you should reply to his request for this information, clearly justifying your reply.

Payment of tax and tax administration

2

Learning outcomes

1.3K	Explain the responsibilities that individuals have for disclosure of income and payment of tax to the relevant tax authorities
1.4K	Explain the main features of the self-assessment system of taxation
1.6K	Identify sources of taxation information for individuals
1.7K	Explain the tax authority's filing and payment process in relation to all personal income
5.1S	Make computations and submissions in accordance with current tax law
5.3S	Apply the due dates of payment of income tax by individuals, including payments on account

Assessment context

Task 6 will test the computation of tax payable and the rules on payment of tax for 10 marks, so you may see some of the contents of this chapter here. Task 7 is a written task for 10 marks requiring you to explain various aspects of the taxation rules, specifically including penalties. There are a lot of very specific rules, dates and percentages in this chapter that could be tested in the exam. Make sure you learn the detail.

Qualification context

You will not see the information in this chapter outside of this unit unless you are also studying *Business Tax*.

Business context

It is vital for a tax adviser to ensure that their client's tax affairs are dealt with in a timely fashion and all information is properly submitted to HMRC. Serious financial penalties will arise if these deadlines are missed.

Chapter overview

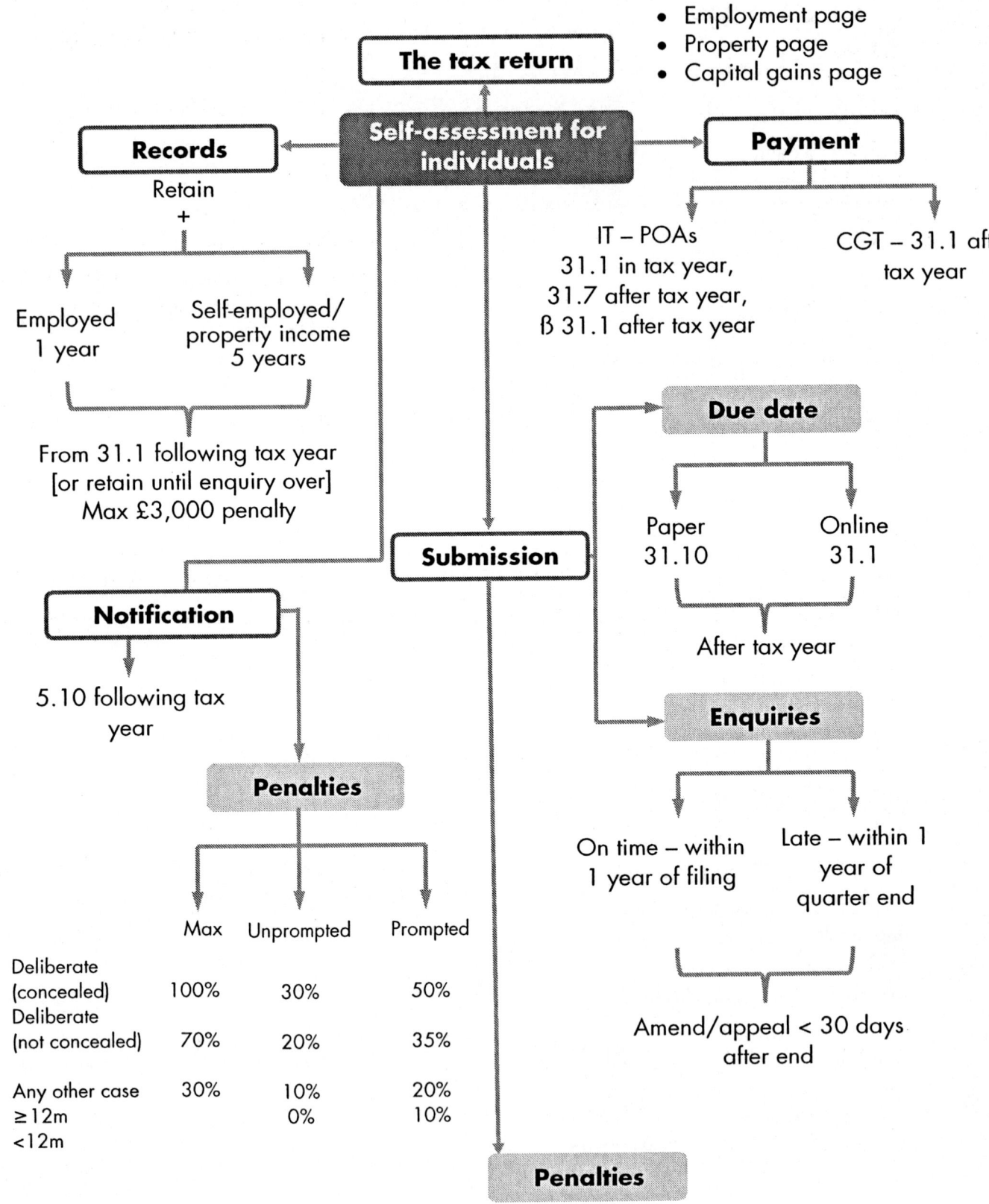

The tax return
- Employment page
- Property page
- Capital gains page

Self-assessment for individuals

Records

Retain
+

Employed
1 year

Self-employed/
property income
5 years

From 31.1 following tax year
[or retain until enquiry over]
Max £3,000 penalty

Notification

5.10 following tax
year

Penalties

	Max	Unprompted	Prompted
Deliberate (concealed)	100%	30%	50%
Deliberate (not concealed)	70%	20%	35%
Any other case	30%	10%	20%
≥12m		0%	10%
<12m			

Payment

IT – POAs
31.1 in tax year,
31.7 after tax year,
ß 31.1 after tax year

CGT – 31.1 after
tax year

Submission

Due date

Paper
31.10

Online
31.1

After tax year

Enquiries

On time – within
1 year of filing

Late – within 1
year of
quarter end

Amend/appeal < 30 days
after end

Penalties

12

BPP
LEARNING MEDIA

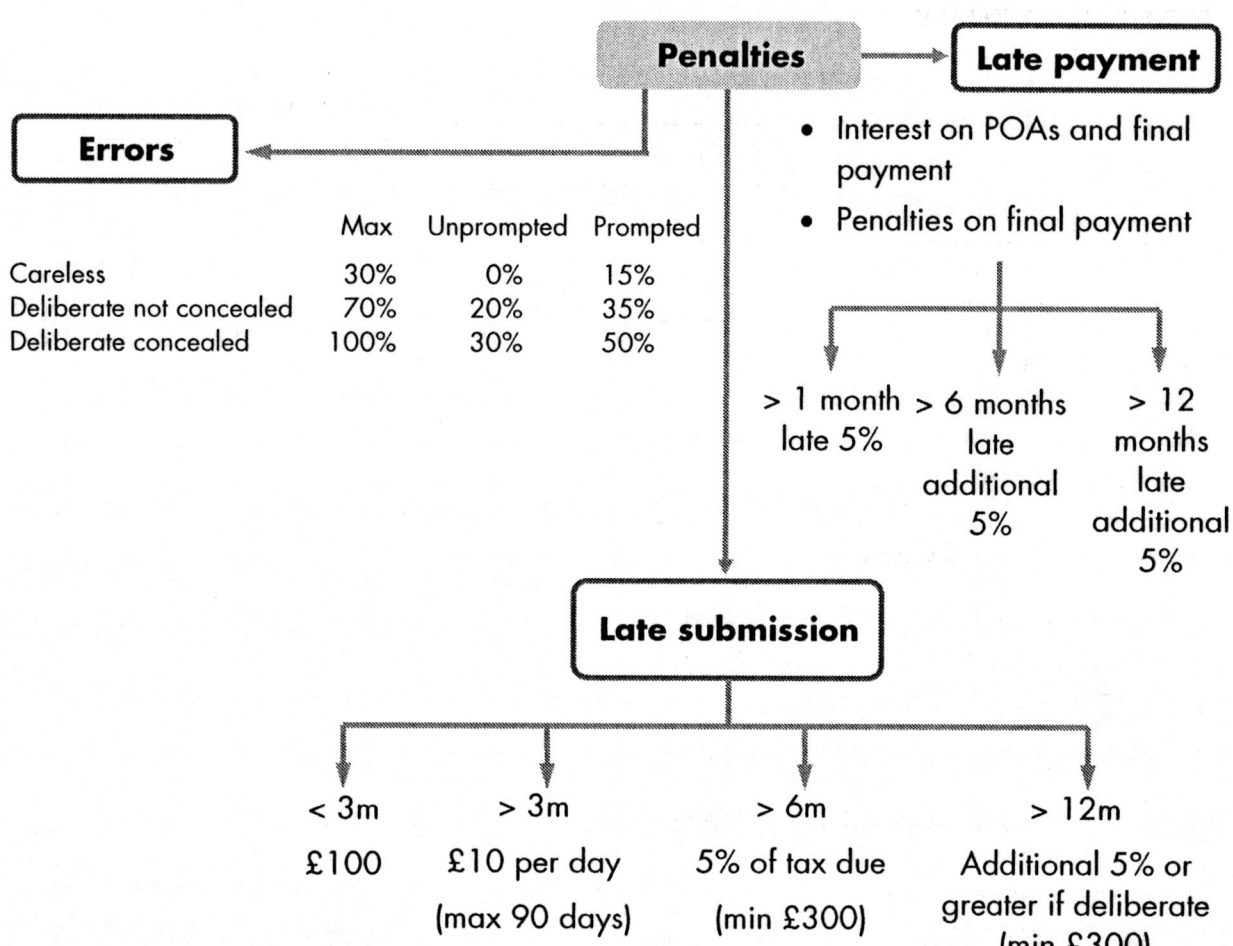

Penalties → **Late payment**

Errors

	Max	Unprompted	Prompted
Careless	30%	0%	15%
Deliberate not concealed	70%	20%	35%
Deliberate concealed	100%	30%	50%

- Interest on POAs and final payment
- Penalties on final payment

> 1 month late 5%	> 6 months late additional 5%	> 12 months late additional 5%

Late submission

< 3m	> 3m	> 6m	> 12m
£100	£10 per day (max 90 days)	5% of tax due (min £300)	Additional 5% or greater if deliberate (min £300)

Introduction

The UK has a self-assessment tax system. That means it is the taxpayer's responsibility to pay the right amount of tax at the right time. If deadlines are not met, payments are made late or errors are included in the tax return then there will be financial penalties. This chapter considers these detailed rules that a tax practitioner must follow on behalf of their client.

1 The tax return

An individual may have to submit a tax return to HMRC informing them of the details of their income for the tax year. An individual's tax return comprises a tax form, together with supplementary pages for particular sources of income and capital gains.

> **Assessment focus point**
>
> In your exam you may have to complete:
>
> - The employment income page;
> - The property income page; or
> - The capital gains tax page.

2 Notice of chargeability

If you have income that needs to be reported on a self-assessment tax return, you have to notify HMRC by 5 October following the tax year in which the income was received.

For 2016/17 the deadline is therefore 5 October 2017.

Employees will generally not have to complete a tax return and all the administration of their taxation including payment will be handled by their employer.

However, if you have other income that is not taxed at source which HMRC is not aware of, such as property income, you will have to notify HMRC.

3 Timetable for 2016/17

31/10/2016	31/1/2017
Filing deadline for paper returns	Filing deadline for online returns
HMRC will calculate tax	Automatic electronic calculation of tax

Where a notice to make a return is issued after 31 July following the tax year a period of three months is allowed for the filing of a paper return.

Where a notice to make a return is issued after 31 October following the tax year a period of three months is allowed for the online filing of that return.

An individual may ask HM Revenue & Customs (HMRC) to make the tax computation if a paper return is filed. Where an online return is filed, the tax computation is made automatically.

Illustration 1: Filing income tax returns

Advise the following clients of the latest filing date for their personal tax return for 2016/17 if notice to file the return is received on the following dates and the return is:

(a) Paper
(b) Online

Notice to file tax return issued by HMRC:

Norma	on 6 April 2017
Melanie	on 10 August 2017
Olga	on 12 December 2017

The latest filing dates are:

	Paper	Online
Norma	31 October 2017	31 January 2018
Melanie	9 November 2017	31 January 2018
Olga	11 March 2018	11 March 2018

---

4 Retention of records

A taxpayer must have records of amounts received, tax deducted and expenses incurred. These records may include:

- Employment income: cash earnings are recorded on Form P60, non-cash benefits on Form P11D. Invoices should be kept to support expense claims.

- Property income: tenancy agreements and receipts for rents received and expenses.

- Savings income: statements of interest received.

- Dividend income: dividend certificates.

- Capital gains: records of original cost, enhancement expenditure.

- General: records of charitable donations and pension contributions made.

All records must be retained until the later of:

- One year following 31 January after the end of the tax year (eg 31 January 2019 for tax year 2016/17) or

- Five years following 31 January after the end of the tax year (eg 31 January 2023 for tax year 2016/17) for taxpayers who are self-employed or have

property income (**Note.** All records must be retained for this time, not just property and self-employment records.)

- Time at which enquiries can no longer be opened (see later)
- Time at which enquiries are concluded

The maximum penalty for failure to keep records is £3,000.

5 Penalties for errors

A penalty may be imposed where a taxpayer makes an inaccurate return if they have:

(a) Been careless because they have not taken reasonable care in making the return or they discover the error later but do not take reasonable steps to inform HMRC

(b) Made a deliberate error but do not make arrangements to conceal it

(c) Made a deliberate error and have attempted to conceal it, eg by submitting false evidence in support of an inaccurate figure

If there is more than one error HMRC may charge more than one penalty.

Penalties may be reduced if the errors are brought to HMRC's attention by the taxpayer.

This could be an unprompted disclosure, where the taxpayer admits the error before HMRC has any knowledge of irregularity, or a prompted disclosure, when the taxpayer suspects the error has been or is about to be discovered.

Potential lost revenue (PLR)	The penalty will be based on the potential lost revenue (PLR). The PLR is the tax that would have been lost if the error had gone undetected.

Penalties are as follows:

Type of error	Maximum penalty	Minimum penalty with prompted disclosure	Minimum penalty with unprompted disclosure
Simple	No penalty	No penalty	No penalty
Careless	30%	15%	0%
Deliberate but not concealed	70%	35%	20%
Deliberate and concealed	100%	50%	30%

The scale of the reduction will vary depending upon the help the taxpayer has given HMRC in respect of:

- Advising about the error, making full disclosure and explaining how it was made

- Assisting HMRC to enable it to quantify the error

- Allowing access to records

A penalty for a careless error may be suspended by HMRC to allow the taxpayer to take action to ensure that the error does not occur again (eg where the error has arisen from failure to keep proper records).

HMRC will impose conditions which the taxpayer has to satisfy, eg establishing proper recordkeeping systems.

The penalty will be cancelled if the conditions imposed by HMRC are complied with by the taxpayer within a period of up to two years.

A taxpayer may appeal against:

- The penalty being charged
- The amount of the penalty
- A decision by HMRC not to suspend a penalty
- Conditions set by HMRC in relation to the suspension of a penalty

Activity 1: Penalties

Kelly deliberately omitted an invoice from her trading income in her 2015/16 tax return, but did not destroy the evidence. She later disclosed this error, before she had reason to believe HMRC might investigate the matter.

Required

Complete the following sentence:

Kelly's penalty can be reduced from [70] % of the potential lost revenue (for a deliberate, but not concealed error) to [20] %, with the unprompted disclosure of her error.

6 Penalties for late notification

A penalty can be charged for failure to notify chargeability to income tax and/or capital gains tax. Penalties are behaviour related, increasing for more serious failures, and are again based on potential lost revenue. This time the PLR is the income tax or capital gains tax which is unpaid on 31 January following the tax year.

The minimum and maximum penalties as percentages of PLR are as follows:

Behaviour	Maximum penalty	Minimum penalty with prompted disclosure		Minimum penalty with unprompted disclosure	
Deliberate and concealed	100%	50%		30%	
Deliberate but not concealed	70%	35%		20%	
		≥12m	<12m	≥12m	<12m
Careless	30%	20%	10%	10%	0%

Penalty may be reduced to 0% if the failure is rectified within 12 months through **unprompted disclosure**.

Penalties may be reduced at HMRC's discretion in special circumstances.

If failure is not deliberate, there is no penalty if the taxpayer has a reasonable excuse. Inability to pay is not a reasonable excuse.

7 Penalties for late filing

The tax return is due by 31 October or 31 January following the tax year depending on whether paper or online return. The penalties for filing a late tax return are:

Return outstanding	Penalty
⟶ 3 months	– £100
3 ⟶ 6 months	– Daily penalty of £10 per day (max 90 days)
6 ⟶ 12 months*	– 5% of the tax due (min £300)
⟶ 12 months*	(i) 100% of the tax due where withholding of information is deliberate and concealed (ii) 70% of the tax due where withholding of information is deliberate but not concealed (iii) 5% of the tax due in other cases (eg careless)

*These tax based penalties are subject to a minimum of £300.

Penalties may be set aside if the taxpayer had a reasonable excuse.

8 Due dates for 2016/17 self-assessed tax

8.1 Income tax

A taxpayer must usually make **three payments of tax**:

Date	Payment
31 January in the tax year	First payment on account
31 July after the tax year	Second payment on account
31 January after the tax year	Final payment to settle any remaining liability

Each **payment on account** (POA) is equal to 50% of the tax liability for the previous year.

If HMRC is late in requesting a tax return then the final payment date is extended to three months following Notice to Deliver date (provided the taxpayer has notified chargeability on time).

POAs may be reduced if the taxpayer expects this year's liability to be lower than last year's. **Interest** will be charged if POAs are reduced and the final tax is greater than expected.

POAs are not required if the income tax payable for the previous year is less than £1,000 or if more than 80% of last year's liability was deducted at source.

Illustration 2: Payments on account

Jameel made payments on account for 2016/17 of £7,500 each on 31 January 2017 and 31 July 2017, based on his 2015/16 tax payable of £15,000. He later calculates his total income tax payable for 2016/17 at £20,000. He also calculates that the capital gains tax payable for 2016/17 is £4,900.

The final payment for 2016/17, payable on 31 January 2018, is calculated as follows:

	£
Income tax (£20,000 – £7,500 – £7,500)	5,000
Capital gains tax	4,900
Final payment	9,900

Note that the first payment on account for the following year (2017/18) would be made on this date too.

The due date for the final payment is normally 31 January following the end of the tax year. However, if the taxpayer has notified chargeability by 5 October but the notice to file a tax return is not issued before 31 October, then the due date for the final payment is three months after the issue of the notice.

8.2 Capital gains tax

Capital gains tax is due on 31 January following the tax year. Capital gains tax is never paid by instalments.

Activity 2: Payments on account and balancing payments

Vorus's tax for 2015/16 was as follows:

	£
Income tax liability	7,000
PAYE	4,000
Capital gains tax	5,000

His tax for 2016/17 is as follows:

	£
Income tax liability	8,000
PAYE	2,500
Capital gains tax	1,000

Required

Complete the following sentences:

His first payment on account is £ [8500] due on [31 Jan 17] (XX/XX/XXXX)

His second payment on account is £ [3500] due on [31 Jul 17] (XX/XX/XXXX)

His final payment is £ [5500] due on [31 Jan 18] (XX/XX/XXXX)

9 Penalties for late payment

Penalties for late payment of tax will be imposed in respect of **balancing payments** of income tax.

A penalty is chargeable where tax is paid after the penalty date. **The penalty date is 30 days after the due date for tax.** Therefore no penalty arises if the tax is paid within 30 days of the due date.

Paid	Penalty
⟶ 30 days	0%
30 days – 6 months	5% of unpaid tax
6 months – 12 months	Further 5% of unpaid tax (10%)
12 months ⟶	Further 5% of unpaid tax (15%)

Penalties for late payment of tax **apply to balancing payments** of income tax. They **do not apply to late payments on account**.

10 Interest

Interest is chargeable on **late payment of both payments on account and balancing payments**. In both cases interest runs from the **due date until the day before the actual date of payment**.

- POAs:
    - From 31 January during tax year
    - From 31 July following end of tax year

- Final payment:
    - From 31 January following end of tax year

If a taxpayer claims to reduce their payments on account and there is still a final payment to be made, interest is normally charged on the payments on account as if each of those payments had been the lower of:

(a) The reduced amount, plus 50% of the final income tax payable

(b) The amount which would have been payable had no claim for reduction been made

11 Repayment of tax and repayment interest

Overpaid tax is repaid unless a greater payment of tax is due in the following 30 days, in which case it is set off against that payment.

Repayment interest is paid on overpayments of:

- Payments on account
- Final payments of tax
- Penalties

Interest runs from the later of the due date and the actual date of payment until the day before repayment is made.

12 Compliance checks and enquiries

Usually under self-assessment HMRC will accept taxpayers' figures.

However, HMRC has the power to conduct a compliance check.

Some returns are selected for a compliance check at random, others for a particular reason; for example, if HMRC believes that there has been an underpayment of tax due to the taxpayer's failure to comply with tax legislation.

There are two types of compliance check:

(1) Pre-return check using information powers
(2) Enquiries into submitted returns

Examples of when a pre-return check may be carried out in practice include:

- To assist with clearances or ruling requests

- Where a previous check has identified poor recordkeeping

- To check that computer systems will produce the information needed to support a return

- To find out about planning or avoidance schemes

- Where fraud is suspected

HMRC must give notice of intention to conduct an enquiry not later than:

- 12 months after filing (if not late) or
- 12 months after quarter end in which return delivered

(Quarters are 31 January, 30 April, 31 July and 31 October if submitted late.)

HMRC has only one opportunity to open a formal enquiry and a tax return cannot be subject to a formal enquiry more than once.

In the course of the enquiries the taxpayer may be required to produce documents, accounts or other information. The taxpayer can appeal to the Tax Tribunal against this.

HMRC must issue a closure notice when the enquiries are complete, state the conclusions and amend the self-assessment accordingly. If the taxpayer is not satisfied with the amendment they may, within 30 days, appeal to the Tax Tribunal.

> **Assessment focus point**
>
> None of the information in this chapter is included within the 'taxation data', which you will be provided with in the live assessment.

Chapter summary

- A tax return must be filed by 31 January following a tax year provided it is filed online. Paper returns must be filed by 31 October following the tax year.

- Taxpayers must keep records until the later of:
  - One year after 31 January following the tax year
  - Five years after 31 January following the tax year if in business or with property income

- A penalty may be imposed if the taxpayer makes an error in their tax return based on the potential lost revenue as a result of the error.

- A penalty may be imposed if the taxpayer does not notify HMRC of their liability to pay income tax or capital gains tax. The penalty is based on potential lost revenue.

- A fixed penalty of £100 applies if a return is filed late, followed by a potential daily penalty of £10 if the return is filed between 3 and 6 months late.

- A tax-geared penalty will also apply if a return is filed more than 6 months late, with a further penalty if this is over 12 months late.

- Payments on account of income tax are required on 31 January in the tax year and on 31 July following the tax year.

- Balancing payments of income tax are due on 31 January following the tax year.

- Late payment penalties apply to balancing payments of income tax. They do not apply to late payments on account.

- Interest is chargeable on late payment of both payments on account and balancing payments.

- HMRC can enquire into a return, usually within one year of receipt of the return.

Keywords

- **Balancing payment:** final payment of tax for the tax year consisting of all outstanding income and capital gains tax following deduction of payments deducted at source and payments on account

- **Interest:** charged on late payments on account and on late balancing payments

- **Payment on account:** an amount paid on account of income tax

- **Penalties for late payment of tax:** penalties levied on late final payments of tax

- **Potential lost revenue:** tax that would have been missed if a failure to notify a new source of income or an error had not been picked up

- **Prompted disclosure:** when a taxpayer brings a matter to the HMRC's attention following communication with HMRC about a related matter

- **Repayment interest:** payable by HMRC on overpaid payments on account, balancing payments and penalties

- **Unprompted disclosure:** when a taxpayer brings a matter to the HMRC's attention without being prompted

Activity answers

Activity 1: Penalties

Kelly's penalty can be reduced from [70%] of the potential lost revenue (for a deliberate, but not concealed error) to [20%], with the unprompted disclosure of her error.

Activity 2: Payments on account and balancing payments

His first payment on account is [£1,500] due on [31/01/2017]

His second payment on account is [£1,500] due on [31/07/2017]

His final payment is [£3,500] due on [31/01/2018]

	£
In 2015/16 the following income tax was subject to self-assessment:	
Income tax payable 7,000 – 4,000 =	3,000
The instalments for 2016/17 are therefore	
31.1.17 ½ × 3,000	1,500
31.7.17 ½ × 3,000	1,500
The final payment is therefore	
Income tax liability	8,000
Less PAYE	(2,500)
Less instalments	(3,000)
	2,500
Capital gains tax liability	1,000
31.1.18 Final payment	3,500

1   **The due filing date for an income tax return for 2016/17 assuming the taxpayer will submit the return online is (insert date as XX/XX/XXXX):**

> 31 Jan 18

2   **Select the correct answers from the picklists provided.**

The 2017/18 payments on account will be calculated as

> 50%

of the income tax payable for

> 2016/17

and will be due on

> 31 Jan 18

and

> 31 Jul 18

Picklist 1	Picklist 2	Picklist 3	Picklist 4
50%	2016/17	1 January 2018	31 July 2018
25%	2015/16	31 January 2017	31 December 2017
100%	2017/18	31 January 2018	31 July 2017

3   A notice requiring a tax return for 2016/17 is issued in April 2017 and the return is filed online in May 2018. All income tax was paid in May 2018. No payments on account were due.

Explain what charges will be made on the taxpayer.

4   Susie filed her 2016/17 tax return online on 28 January 2018.

By what date must HMRC give notice that it is going to enquire into the return?

Tick ONE box.

	✓
31 January 2019	
31 March 2019	
6 April 2019	
28 January 2019	✓

5   Jamie paid income tax of £12,000 for 2015/16. In 2016/17, his tax payable was £16,000.

Jamie's 2016/17 payments on account will each be

| 4,000 |

and will be due on **(insert date as XX/XX/XXXX)**

| 31 Jan 18 |

and

| 31 Jul 18 |

Jamie's balancing payment will be

| |

and will be due on **(insert date as XX/XX/XXXX)**

| 31 Jan 19 |

6   Tim should have made 2 payments on account of his 2016/17 income tax payable of £5,000 each. He actually made both of these payments on 31 August 2017.

State the amount of any penalties for late payment.

| £ | |

7   (a)   By what date must a taxpayer generally submit a tax return for 2016/17 if it is filed as a paper return?

Tick ONE box.

	✓
30 September 2017	
31 October 2017	V
31 December 2017	
31 January 2018	

(b)   On which dates are payment on accounts due for 2016/17?

Tick ONE box.

	✓
31 January 2018 and 31 July 2018	V
31 January 2017 and 31 July 2017	
31 October 2017 and 31 January 2018	
31 July 2017 and 31 January 2018	

8 Lola accidentally fails to include property income of £17,000 on her 2016/17 tax return. She pays basic rate tax at 20%, and has not yet disclosed this error.

Identify the maximum penalty that could be imposed on her for the error in her return.

Tick ONE box.

	✓
£5,100	
£3,400	
£1,020	
£2,380	

Employment income

3

Learning outcomes

1.1K	Explain the main current legislation relating to personal taxation
1.2K	Explain the main legislative features relating to income from employment
2.1S	Prepare computations of emoluments, including benefits in kind
2.4K	Describe taxable and non-taxable sources of income from employment, including benefits in kind
3.1S	Apply allowances that can be set against non-savings income
3.2S	Apply deductions and reliefs and claim loss set-offs
3.5S	Describe taxation relief which can be given on income from employment including deductible (allowable) expenses, pension's relief and charitable donations
5.1S	Make computations and submissions in accordance with current tax law

Assessment context

Benefits are highly examinable. Make sure you can calculate and explain them. Task 1 of your CBT specifically tests the rules on car benefits for 9 marks. Task 2 will test other benefits for 10 marks. Task 5 requires you to calculate taxable income for 12 marks, so may pull in some employment income rules. Task 7 requires you to explain an aspect of the tax legislation for 10 marks, so this could test rules from this chapter. You will have to complete a tax return in Task 8 for 7 marks. This could be the employment income page.

Qualification context

You will not see the information in this chapter outside of this unit.

Business context

You will not see these areas again in your AAT qualification outside of this unit.

Chapter overview

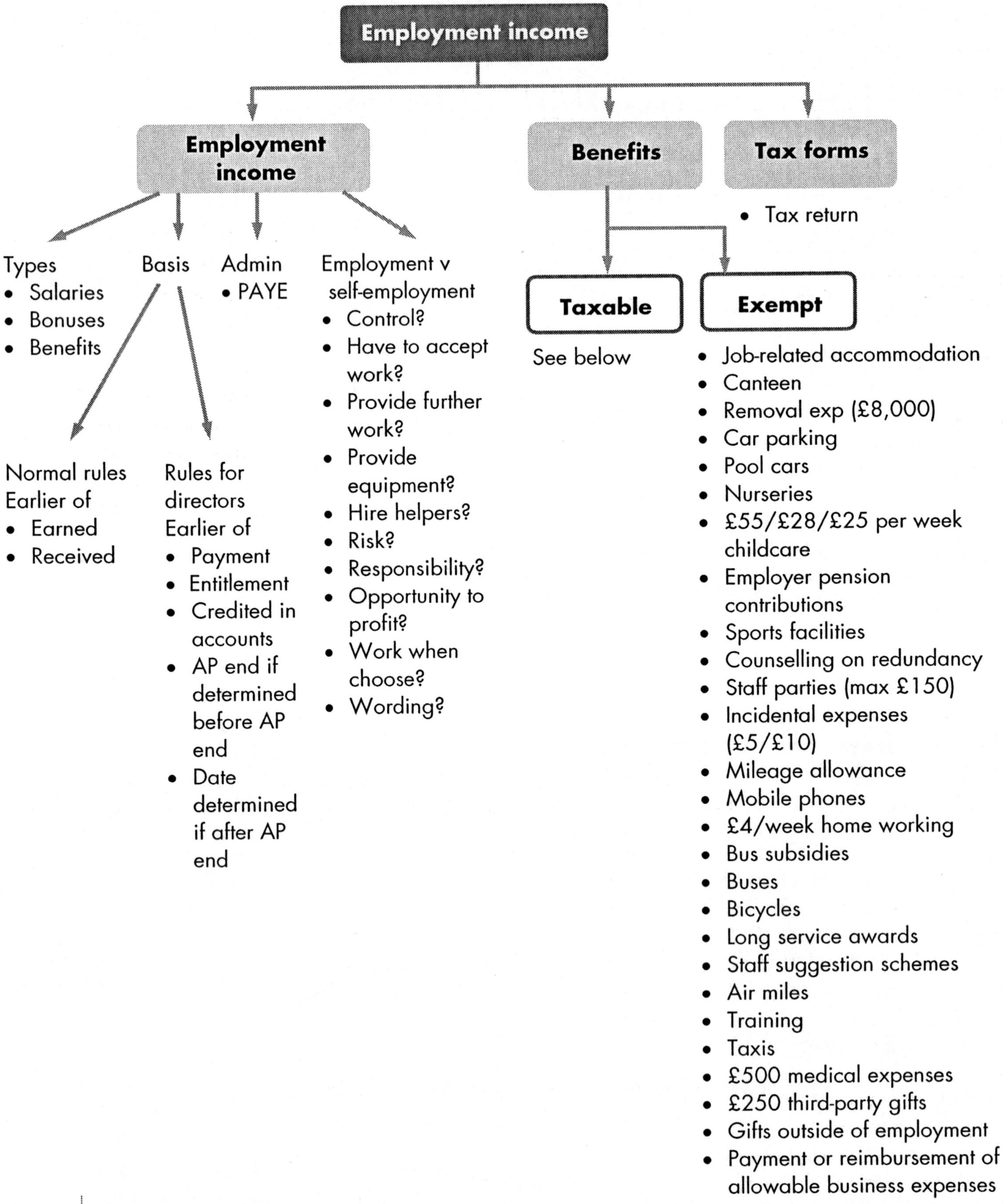

Employment income

Employment income

Types
- Salaries
- Bonuses
- Benefits

Basis

Admin
- PAYE

Employment v self-employment
- Control?
- Have to accept work?
- Provide further work?
- Provide equipment?
- Hire helpers?
- Risk?
- Responsibility?
- Opportunity to profit?
- Work when choose?
- Wording?

Normal rules
Earlier of
- Earned
- Received

Rules for directors
Earlier of
- Payment
- Entitlement
- Credited in accounts
- AP end if determined before AP end
- Date determined if after AP end

Benefits

Tax forms
- Tax return

Taxable
See below

Exempt
- Job-related accommodation
- Canteen
- Removal exp (£8,000)
- Car parking
- Pool cars
- Nurseries
- £55/£28/£25 per week childcare
- Employer pension contributions
- Sports facilities
- Counselling on redundancy
- Staff parties (max £150)
- Incidental expenses (£5/£10)
- Mileage allowance
- Mobile phones
- £4/week home working
- Bus subsidies
- Buses
- Bicycles
- Long service awards
- Staff suggestion schemes
- Air miles
- Training
- Taxis
- £500 medical expenses
- £250 third-party gifts
- Gifts outside of employment
- Payment or reimbursement of allowable business expenses

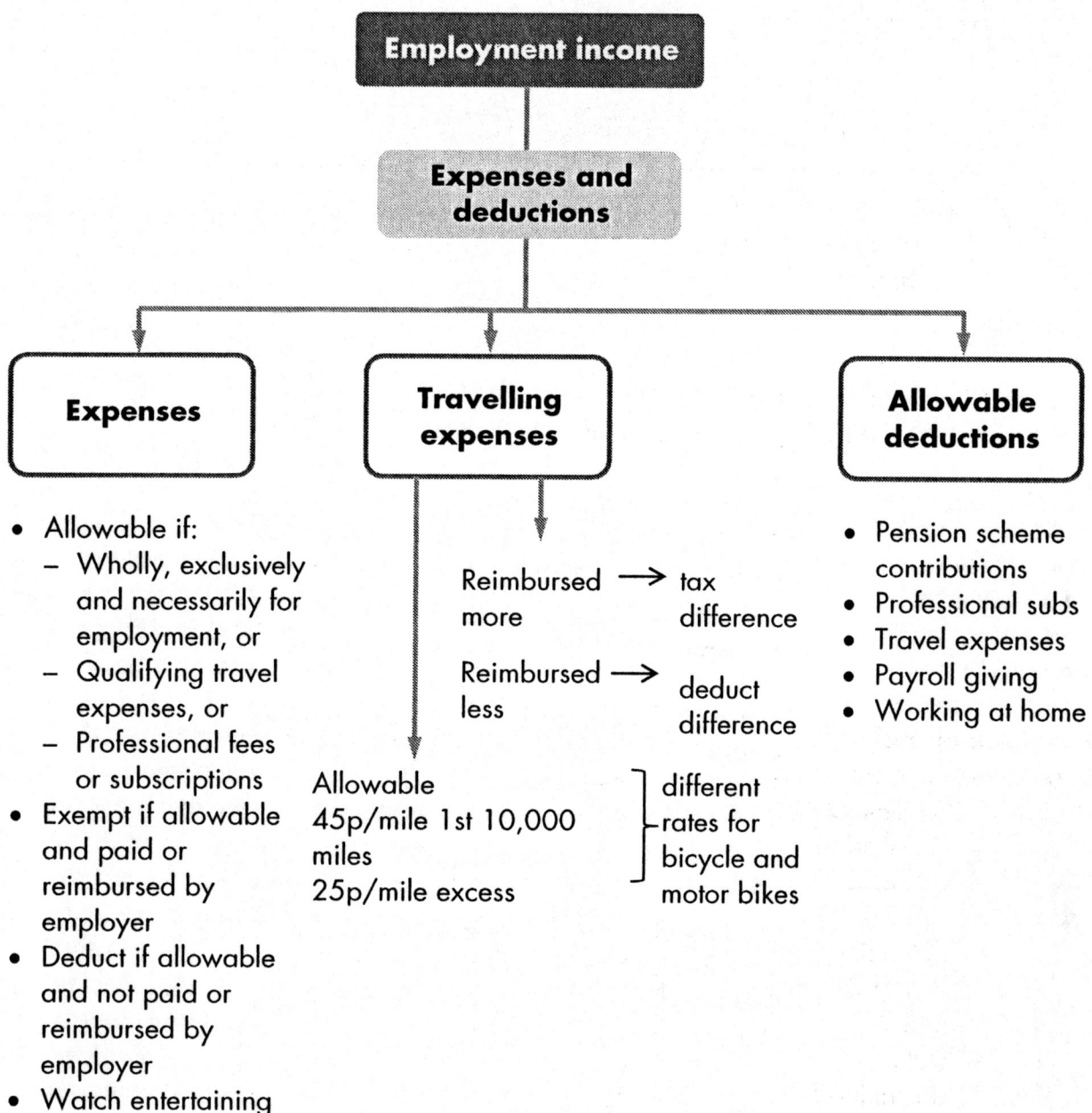

Employment income

Expenses and deductions

Expenses

- Allowable if:
  - Wholly, exclusively and necessarily for employment, or
  - Qualifying travel expenses, or
  - Professional fees or subscriptions
- Exempt if allowable and paid or reimbursed by employer
- Deduct if allowable and not paid or reimbursed by employer
- Watch entertaining

Travelling expenses

Reimbursed more → tax difference

Reimbursed less → deduct difference

Allowable
45p/mile 1st 10,000 miles
25p/mile excess

] different rates for bicycle and motor bikes

Allowable deductions

- Pension scheme contributions
- Professional subs
- Travel expenses
- Payroll giving
- Working at home

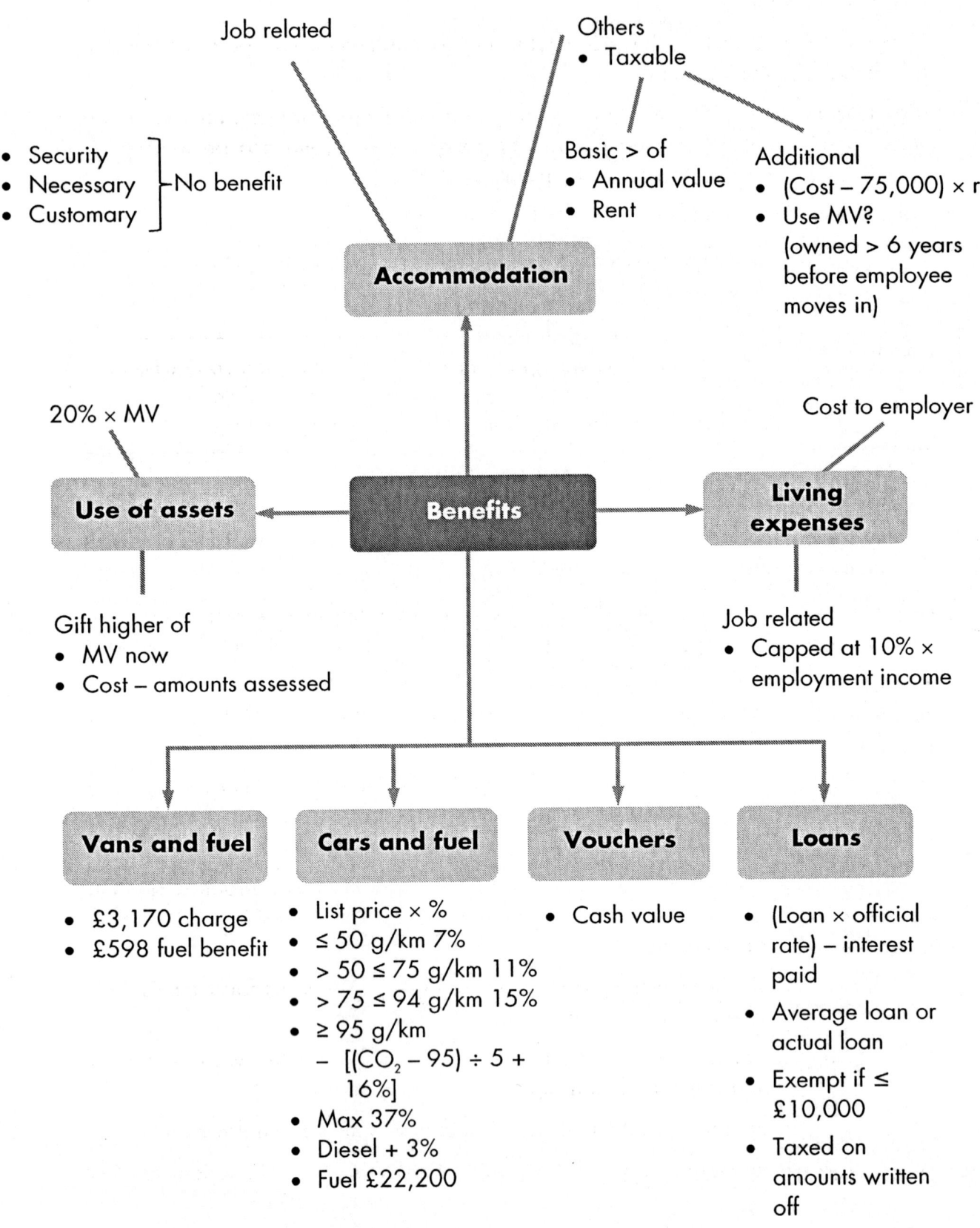

Job related

Others
- Taxable

Security
Necessary   — No benefit
Customary

Basic > of
- Annual value
- Rent

Additional
- (Cost – 75,000) × r
- Use MV? (owned > 6 years before employee moves in)

Accommodation

20% × MV

Use of assets

Benefits

Gift higher of
- MV now
- Cost – amounts assessed

Cost to employer

Living expenses

Job related
- Capped at 10% × employment income

Vans and fuel

- £3,170 charge
- £598 fuel benefit

Cars and fuel

- List price × %
- ≤ 50 g/km 7%
- > 50 ≤ 75 g/km 11%
- > 75 ≤ 94 g/km 15%
- ≥ 95 g/km
  - [(CO_2 – 95) ÷ 5 + 16%]
- Max 37%
- Diesel + 3%
- Fuel £22,200

Vouchers

- Cash value

Loans

- (Loan × official rate) – interest paid
- Average loan or actual loan
- Exempt if ≤ £10,000
- Taxed on amounts written off

Introduction

Before we can calculate the income tax that an individual will pay we have to calculate their total income.

Their total income will be made up of income from different sources; for example a person renting out property will have **property income**, while a person who is employed will have **employment income**.

Different types of income are calculated in different ways.

In this chapter we are going to look at how to calculate employment income.

1 Employment income

Key term

Employment income	This is the type of income received by someone who holds an office or employment. It is calculated using the detailed rules we will be considering in this chapter.

It is usually clear whether someone is employed or self-employed. If you work for the same person every working day for a regular salary then you are employed. If you pay, say, a plumber to perform some work for you then they are self-employed; they are not your employee.

However, in certain circumstances it is not obvious whether a taxpayer is an employee or self-employed. It is important to classify the relationship correctly otherwise the wrong tax rules would be applied.

HMRC would consider whether the taxpayer has a **contract of service** or **a contract for services**.

A contract of service means the taxpayer works for the other party over a period of time, performing different tasks as they are assigned to them. The relationship is ongoing. This makes them employed.

A contract for services means the taxpayer has agreed to perform a specific task or tasks. Once these tasks have been completed the relationship is at an end. This makes them self-employed.

If it is not clear whether we have a contract of service or contract for services then HMRC would consider the following:

(a) The degree of control exercised over the person doing the work – control implies an employment relationship

(b) Whether they must accept further work – obligation implies employment

(c) Whether the other party must provide further work – obligation implies employment

(d) Whether they provide their own equipment – using someone else's equipment implies an employment relationship

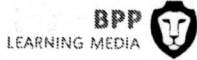

(e) Whether they hire their own helpers – hiring their own helpers suggests autonomy meaning they are self-employed

(f) What degree of financial risk they take – self-employment is more risky than employment

(g) What degree of responsibility for investment and management they have – self-employed people have more responsibility than employed people

(h) Whether they can profit from sound management – self-employed people will benefit directly from good decisions they make

(i) Whether they can work when they choose – self-employed people have more flexibility over how they work

(j) The wording used in any agreement between the parties – this will help us to understand the nature of the relationship

In this unit we are only concerned with the taxation of employed people. The calculation of income from self-employment is a major part of the *Business Tax* syllabus.

2 Taxation of employment income

2.1 Types of income

A taxpayer will be taxed on any amounts deriving from an office or employment performed wholly or partly in the UK including:

- Salaries, bonuses and commissions
- Non-cash benefits, for example a company car
- Payments made on termination of employment

2.2 Basis of assessment

These rules identify the tax year that income is taxed in. There are normal rules and additional rules that apply to directors only.

2.2.1 Normal rules

A taxpayer will be assessed on amounts received in the current tax year (6 April 2016 – 5 April 2017).

Earnings are treated as received at the earlier of:

- The time when payment is made
- The time when a person becomes entitled to payment of the earnings

Illustration 1: Basis of assessment

Joy is employed by R plc. She is entitled to the payment of a bonus of £2,000 on 31 March 2017, although she does not receive it until 25 April 2017.

Joy will be taxed on the bonus in 2016/17 because she is entitled to payment on 31 March 2017.

Activity 1: Basis of assessment

Rudolph is an employee of Mabuse Ltd. He earns a salary of £28,000 but on 1 November 2016 he is promoted and his salary increases to £35,000. The company also pays him a bonus relating to the year ended 31 March 2016 of £3,000 on 15 May 2016. The bonus for the year ended 31 March 2017 of £4,000 is paid on 13 May 2017.

Required

(a) What is Rudolph's taxable salary for 2016/17?

£ `30916` $28,000 \times \frac{7}{12} = 16,333$ $+14,583$ $+3,000$ $+4,000$

(b) What is Rudolph's taxable bonus for 2016/17?

£ `3,000`

2.2.2 Rules for directors

Special rules apply to company directors. Their earnings are treated as being received on the earliest of:

- The time when payment is made

- The time when a person becomes entitled to payment of the earnings

- The time when the amount is credited in the company's accounting records

- The end of the company's period of account (if the amount has been determined by then)

- The time the amount is determined (if after the end of the company's period of account)

2.3 Deduction of tax by employers

Employers have an obligation to deduct income tax from payments they make to their employees under the **Pay As You Earn (PAYE) system**. Tax is deducted on both cash payments and benefits. Employees therefore receive their salary net of tax.

Most employees will have the correct amount of tax deducted by their employers so there will be no need for them to complete a tax return or make further payments of tax.

In your assessment salaries will be quoted gross. This means you are given the figure before tax has been deducted. You will then be provided with information as to the amount of income tax deducted under PAYE.

3 Taxable benefits

Certain perks provided by employers represent **benefits** taxable on employees. The rules on these are set out in legislation called the **benefits code**.

There are specific rules applying to certain benefits, for example cars. If there is no specific rule then employees will be taxed on the cost to the employer of providing the benefit.

As a general rule:

- There is no taxable benefit if there is no private benefit to the employee (eg no benefit for the use of a projector in class by a BPP tutor)

- Time apportion the benefit if it is not available for the whole tax year

- Deduct any contributions made by the employee from the benefit

3.1 Cars

A car provided by the employer that is available for private use gives rise to a benefit. If fuel is provided for private motoring there will be an additional benefit.

Note that HMRC considers commuting to work and back as private use so in practice if an employee uses a car belonging to their employer they will normally be taxed on this as a benefit. The exception to this would be a **pool car** (see later).

3.1.1 Car benefit

The starting point for calculating a car benefit is the list price of the car. A percentage of that list price is the taxable benefit.

The price of the car is calculated as follows:

- List price when new, plus optional extras costing at least £100
- Deduct capital contributions made by employee (capped at £5,000)

The percentage used varies, depending on the CO_2 emissions and whether the car is petrol- or diesel-fuelled:

Assessment focus point

CO_2 g/km	Petrol engine	Diesel engine
≤ 50 g/km	7%	10%
> 50 ≤ 75 g/km	11%	14%
> 75 ≤ 94 g/km	15%	18%
≥ 95 g/km	Calculation • Minimum 16% • Maximum 37%	Calculation • Minimum 19% • Maximum 37%

The rate for electric cars is always 7%.

Formula provided

For cars that emit CO_2 of more than 94 g/km, the taxable benefit percentage starts at 16% and increases by 1% for every 5 g/km (rounded down to the nearest multiple of 5) by which CO_2 emissions exceed 95 g/km, up to a maximum of 37%.

Illustration 2: Car benefit percentage

Working for a car with CO_2 emissions > 94 g/km

The relevant CO_2 percentage for a petrol car with 187 g/km CO_2 emissions is calculated as follows:

Round down to 185

185 – 95 = 90

Divided by 5 = 18

Add basic 18 + 16 = 34%

Diesel cars have a supplement of 3%. The maximum benefit, however, remains 37% of the list price.

The benefit is apportioned if the car is not available for the whole year or cannot be used for a period of at least 30 days (for example if being repaired).

The benefit is reduced by any payment the user must make for the private use of the car (as distinct from a one-off capital contribution to the cost of the car which would be deducted from the price before applying the percentage).

Pool cars are exempt. A car is a pool car if all the following conditions are satisfied:

- It is used by more than one employee/director and not ordinarily used by one of them to the exclusion of others.

- Any private use is incidental to business use.

- Not normally kept overnight at or near the residence of an employee.

3.1.2 Fuel benefit

Where fuel is provided for private miles (including commuting) there is a further benefit in addition to the car benefit.

The taxable benefit is a percentage of a base figure. The base figure for 2016/17 is £22,200 (see tax tables).

The percentage is the same percentage as is used to calculate the car benefit.

Assessment focus point

Exceptionally there is no reduction in benefit for contributions made by the employee – don't get caught out by this!

There is no benefit if the employee pays for all private fuel.

Illustration 3: Car and fuel benefit

An employee was provided with a new petrol engine car costing £15,000 (the list price) on 6 June 2016. During 2016/17, the employer spent £900 on insurance, repairs and the vehicle licence. The firm paid for all petrol (£2,300) without reimbursement. The employee was required to pay the firm £25 per month for the private use of the car. The car has CO_2 emissions of 84 g/km.

The total taxable benefit for 2016/17 in respect of the car and fuel is calculated as follows:

	£
List price £15,000 × 15%	2,250
£2,250 × 10/12	1,875
Less contribution (10 × £25)	(250)
	1,625
Fuel benefit £22,200 × 15% × 10/12	2,775
Total taxable benefit	4,400

If the contribution of £25 per month had been towards the petrol, the contribution would not be deducted, making the benefit assessable £250 greater. Conversely, if the cost of private petrol was fully reimbursed by the employee, then there would have been no fuel benefit at all.

Activity 2: Car and fuel benefit

Damon who works for Stuart Ltd earns £50,000 (PAYE £21,000) and has use of a company car, a Jaguar S-Type 2.5 (brand new). The CO_2 emissions rate is 169 g/km. The car has a list price of £60,000 but the employer negotiated a discount and bought it for £57,000. The company fitted accessories (CD player and child safety seat) at a cost of £900.

Damon is required to pay £100 per month towards the running costs of the car (excluding petrol). The company meets all Damon's petrol costs in 2016/17 which amounted to £3,500.

Required

(a) **What is Damon's taxable benefit for 2016/17?**

£ [   ]

(b) **What is the benefit if Damon left the company on 1 January 2017 and returned the car on that date?**

£ [   ]

3.2 Vans

There is a £3,170 charge when vans are available to employees for private use.

Assessment focus point

Note that, unlike company cars, a home to work journey does not qualify as private use for a van.

If the van has CO_2 emissions of 0, then the benefit is 20% of the normal benefit ie £634.

There is an additional £598 charge if fuel is made available for private use.

3.3 Other assets

The following rules apply if any other asset is provided to an employee.

3.3.1 Use of asset

Formula to learn

If an employee is allowed to use an asset owned by their employer for private purposes they will be assessed on the higher of:

- 20% of the value when first made available to employee
- Rental paid by employer

3.3.2 Gift of asset

Formula to learn

If an employee is given an asset that previously belonged to their employer they will be assessed as follows:

- If already used by employee, the higher of:
  - Market value when given
  - Original value when first used less values already assessed
- If a new asset is given, then the employee will be assessed on the cost of providing the asset
- If the asset is a computer, the benefit can only be current market value
- Deduct from the benefit any payment the employee makes for the asset

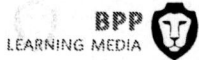

Illustration 4: Use and gift of asset

A suit costing £200 is bought by an employer for use by an employee on 6 April 2015. On 6 April 2016, the suit is purchased by the employee for £15, its market value then being £25.

The benefit taxable in 2015/16 will be 20% × £200 = £40

The benefit taxable in 2016/17 will be the greater of:

(a) Market value at acquisition by employee = £25

(b)

	£	£
Original market value	200	
Less assessed in respect of use 2015/16	(40)	
	160	
Therefore (b)		160
Less price paid by employee		(15)
Taxable benefit 2016/17		145

Activity 3: Use and gift of employer's asset

Gustav Holst, an employee, was given the use of some video equipment on 6 October 2014, when it had a value of £1,000. On 6 January 2017, he was given the asset outright when it was worth £500.

Required

Complete the following sentences:

In 2016/17, his benefit for the use of the asset is   £ ☐

In 2016/17, his benefit on the gift of the asset is   £ ☐

3.4 Beneficial loans

There is a benefit when an employer gives an employee an interest-free loan or when the employer charges less than a commercial interest rate.

The benefit is the difference between the interest that should have been charged, using the official rate of interest (given in the exam), and the interest paid by the employee.

Formula to learn

Where the size of the loan has changed during the year, the interest is calculated on either following:

- The average loan outstanding in the year
- The loan outstanding on a month by month basis

The average method is usually used but either the taxpayer or HMRC can elect to use the month by month calculation.

There is no benefit if the total of all loans made to the employee in the year is £10,000 or less. If this limit is broken then all loans are taxed, not just the excess over £10,000.

An employee will always be taxed on the value of a loan written off by the employer even if the loan was below the £10,000 limit.

Illustration 5: Beneficial loan

At 6 April 2016, a low interest loan of £30,000 was outstanding to a director, who repaid £20,000 on 6 January 2017. The remaining balance of £10,000 was outstanding at 5 April 2017. Interest paid during the year was £250.

The benefit under both methods for 2016/17, assuming that the official rate of interest was 3% throughout 2016/17, is calculated as follows:

Average method

	£
$3\% \times \dfrac{(30,000 + 10,000)}{2}$	600
Less interest paid	(250)
Taxable benefit	350

Alternative method

	£
£30,000 × 9/12 × 3%	675
(6 April 2016 – 6 January 2017)	
£10,000 × 3/12 × 3%	75
(7 January 2017 – 5 April 2017)	
	750
Less interest paid	(250)
Taxable benefit	500

Therefore, the taxable benefit will be £350.

Activity 4: Beneficial loan

At 6 April 2016, a taxable cheap loan of £30,000 was outstanding to an employee earning £12,000 a year, who repaid £20,000 on 7 December 2016. The remaining balance of £10,000 was outstanding at 5 April 2017. Interest paid during the year was £250.

The official rate of interest was 3%.

Required

Complete the following sentences:

The benefit calculated under the average method is £ ☐

The benefit calculated under the strict method is £ ☐

The taxpayer would be taxed on £ ☐

3.5 Accommodation

3.5.1 Job-related accommodation

An employee who is provided with **job-related accommodation** will not be taxed on it under the benefit rules.

Key term

Job-related accommodation	• Provided for security reasons, for example for the Prime Minister; or
	• Necessary for the proper performance of duties, for example a caretaker; or
	• Customary for that sort of work and ensures better performance of duties, for example a pub landlord would traditionally be provided with accommodation.

3.5.2 Accommodation that is not job related

If the accommodation is not job-related, then a taxable benefit arises on employees and is calculated in two stages:

(1) The basic charge is calculated as:

Formula to learn

Basic charge – greater of:

• Annual value
• Rent paid by employer

Illustration 6: Accommodation rented by employer

Tony is provided with a company flat:

	£
Annual value	3,000
Rent paid by the company	3,380
Amount paid by Tony to the company for the use of the flat	520

Tony's taxable benefit is:

Benefit: greater of:		£
(a)	Annual value	3,000
(b)	Rent paid by the company	3,380
Therefore		3,380
Less reimbursed to the company		(520)
Net benefit		2,860

(2) There is an additional charge if the employer owns the building and the cost of the property is greater than £75,000. This is calculated as:

Formula to learn

Accommodation additional charge: (Cost – 75,000) × official rate of interest

Illustration 7: Accommodation owned by employer

Simon's employer provided him with a house throughout 2016/17. The company bought the house for £133,000 on 1 April 2012.

For 2016/17, the annual value of the house is £1,400. Simon pays £3,000 for the use of the house to his employer.

The total benefit arising in respect of the house for 2016/17, assuming the official rate of interest is 3%, is:

Basic charge:

		£
Annual value		1,400
Less Simon's contribution		(1,400)
		Nil

Additional charge:

	£	£
Cost	133,000	
Less	(75,000)	
Excess		58,000
£58,000 × 3%		1,740
Less Simon's contribution (£3,000 – 1,400)		(1,600)
Total benefit 2016/17		140

(3) If the accommodation was acquired more than six years before it was provided to an employee, then the additional charge is based on the market value at the start of the tax year in which the employee moves in.

Activity 5: Accommodation benefit

Ralph has the use of a house belonging to his employer, for which he pays a nominal rent of £2,500. The annual value is £3,000. Ralph has lived in the house since October 2000. It had cost the company £175,000 in October 1999 but is now worth £300,000.

Take the official rate of interest at 3%.

Required

(a) **What is the benefit if the accommodation is job related?**

£ _____

(b) **What is the benefit if the accommodation is not job related?**

£ _____

(c) **What is the benefit if the accommodation is not job related but was bought in October 1992?**

£ _____

3.5.3 Accommodation living expenses

A benefit arises on an employee if their household living expenses are paid for by their employer.

The benefit depends on the accommodation provided:

Formula to learn

- Job-related accommodation:

  Lower of

  - Cost of expenses to employer
  - 10% × net earnings (ie employment income including all other benefits)

- Not job related:

  - Cost of expenses to employer

Expenses include the following items:

- Heating, lighting, cleaning etc
- Repairing, maintaining or decorating
- Providing furniture (annual value taken as 20% of cost)

Activity 6: Accommodation living expenses

Maggie lives in accommodation provided by her employer and her salary is £7,000 per year. Household expenses of £1,800 are paid by her employer and she has other benefits totalling £2,000.

Required

Complete the following sentences:

If the property is 'job related' her benefit is £ ☐

If the property is not 'job related' her benefit is £ ☐

3.6 Vouchers

The employee is normally taxed on the cost incurred by the employer in providing a voucher or credit token (for example a credit card).

If the employee receives a cash voucher, a voucher that can be exchanged for cash, they are taxed on the amount that the voucher can be exchanged for.

Certain vouchers are exempt (see below).

4 Exempt benefits

The following benefits are not taxable. Learn these.

(a) Job-related accommodation.

(b) Canteen offering free or discounted food available to all staff. A benefit would arise if the canteen was only available to selected staff members. The benefit would be the cost to the company net of payments made by the employee.

(c) Qualifying removal expenses up to £8,000 when the employee has to move house because of their job. Qualifying costs include legal and removal costs as well as purchasing replacement goods such as curtains and carpets. Excess payments over the £8,000 would be taxable.

(d) Car parking spaces near place of work.

(e) Occasional taxi fares home where employees are required to work late after 9:00pm.

(f) Use of pool cars.

(g) Workplace nurseries (crèches). The crèche must be operated by the employer.

(h) If the employer pays for the worker's childcare provided by an external provider then some of the payment will be tax free but any excess over a weekly threshold will be taxable. The employer could pay the childcare provider directly or give the employee vouchers. The limits are £55 per week for a basic rate taxpayer, £28 for a higher rate taxpayer and £25 per week for an additional rate taxpayer.

(i) Contributions by an employer into an approved pension scheme.

(j) Sport and recreational facilities available generally for the staff. These must be provided directly by the employer. If the employer pays for facilities provided by an external supplier then this will create a taxable benefit.

(k) Outplacement counselling services to employees made redundant who have been employed full-time for at least two years. The services can include counselling to help adjust to the loss of the job and to help in finding other work.

(l) Annual staff events up to a maximum of £150 per head. If this limit is exceeded then the full cost is taxable.

(m) Incidental expense of £5 per night if working away from home (telephone calls, laundry etc). The limit is £10 if working abroad. These amounts may be aggregated if working away a number of days; for example, if working away for 3 days then the limit for the period would be £15.

(n) Mileage allowances (see later).

(o) Mobile phones – these are exempt if a single phone is provided. A benefit would apply to additional phones provided to the employee.

(p) £4 per week may be paid tax free to cover the cost of home working when the employee is required to work from home. Greater amounts may be claimed if the taxpayer can produce evidence of the actual costs incurred by working from home.

(q) Subsidies paid to bus services used by employees for commuting.

(r) Provision of buses for nine or more employees for commuting.

(s) Provision of bicycles and cycling safety equipment for commuting.

(t) Non-cash gifts given to employees as a reward for service in excess of 20 years are exempt provided the cost is no more than £50 per year worked.

(u)   Awards under staff suggestion schemes.

(v)   Air miles obtained by business travel.

(w)   Work-related training.

(x)   Medical treatment of up to £500 to assist an employee to return to work.

(y)   'Goodwill' gifts of up to £250 from a single third party.

(z)   Gifts made to employees outside of employment, for example a marriage gift.

5 Allowable deductions

Certain expenses may be deducted from employment income before tax is applied.

Assessment focus point

The general rule for allowable deductions states that expenses must be incurred **'wholly, exclusively and necessarily'** (HMRC, 2014) in the performance of duties. This means that if the employee could perform their duties without incurring the expense then it is not deductible as it is not strictly necessary.

The following are specific allowable deductions:

- Fees and subscriptions to relevant professional bodies

- Travelling and other expenses incurred in the performance of duties

- Contributions to an approved occupational pension scheme, an occupational scheme is one provided by the employer

- Donations to charity under **payroll deduction scheme**

- £4 per week deduction to cover household expenses incurred when working at home

5.1 Expenses

Employees will incur expenditure performing their job. They may or may not be reimbursed by their employer for these expenses. Certain business expenses are allowable:

- Wholly, exclusively and necessarily incurred in the performance of the duties of the employment, or

- Qualifying travel expenses (see 5.1.4), or

- Professional fees and subscriptions

The treatment of these expenses depends upon whether the employee is reimbursed for the expenditure by their employer or not.

5.1.1 Employee incurs expenditure without reimbursement

If the employee bears the cost of the expense themselves without reimbursement from their employer then they would simply deduct the expense from their employment income.

Illustration 8: Expenses not reimbursed

Paul earns a salary of £35,000 a year. He has to pay his £500 subscription to the Chartered Institute of Taxation. Paul's employer does not reimburse him for this expense.

Paul's employment income calculation would be as follows:

	£
Salary	35,000
Less expenses	(500)
Employment income	34,500

5.1.2 Employee incurs expenditure and is reimbursed by employer, or employer pays directly

From 2016/17 the payment or reimbursement of expenses is exempt (ie no need to include in earnings) if they are fully allowable and the employee would therefore otherwise be able to claim a deduction. Employers will no longer be required to apply for a dispensation. This makes the administration of such expenses far simpler.

Illustration 9: Reimbursed expenses

Paul earns a salary of £35,000 a year. His employer reimburses him for his £500 subscription to the Chartered Institute of Taxation.

The subscription is exempt income as it is a reimbursed allowable expense, so it is not included in the calculations of earnings.

	£
Salary	35,000
Reimbursed expenses (exempt)	nil
Employment income	35,000

5.1.3 Expenses with a private and business element

Strictly, if an expense has a 'private' and 'business' component, then it is not exclusively used in the duties of employment and will not be allowed (for example if a phone is used for work purposes and privately, then no deduction can be claimed for the line rental, although the cost of the business calls would be allowed).

In practice, HMRC will allow taxpayers to apportion costs where there is a business and a private element. The business use will be an allowable expense, and

deductible for the employee on their tax return. If the allowable element is clearly identifiable, the exemption will apply.

5.1.4 Travel expenses

Travelling expenses are deductible; if the employer reimburses this is an exempt benefit. As noted above, if expenses are not reimbursed then the taxpayer may deduct the expense.

Only business travelling is allowable. Normal commuting from home to office is excluded.

An exception is where an employee is seconded to a **temporary workplace** for less than 24 months; here commuting from home is allowable.

5.1.5 Approved mileage allowance payments

Employers may reimburse employees for using their own car on their employer's business. The reimbursement is to cover fuel and all other costs associated with using the car, for example depreciation, road tax and insurance.

Formula provided

The allowable limits are:

- 45p per mile for the first 10,000 miles per tax year
- 25p per mile for the excess

If the employer pays more than the permitted amount, the excess is taxable.

If the employer pays less than the permitted amount, the employee can deduct the difference from their earnings.

There are separate rates for motorcycles and bicycles. These would be given to you in the exam.

Illustration 10: Statutory mileage

Owen drives 14,000 business miles in 2016/17 using his own car.

You are required to calculate the taxable benefit/allowable deduction assuming:

(a) He is reimbursed 45p a mile
(b) He is reimbursed 25p a mile

	£
Statutory limit: 10,000 × 45p	4,500
4,000 × 25p	1,000
	5,500

(a)

	£
Amount received (14,000 × 45p)	6,300
Less statutory limit	(5,500)
Taxable benefit	800

(b)

	£
Amount received (14,000 × 25p)	3,500
Less statutory limit	(5,500)
Allowable deduction	(2,000)

Activity 7: Statutory mileage

Jen drives 15,000 miles in the tax year.

Required

(a) **Choose the correct option and insert the numerical value.**

If Jen's employer pays her 30p per mile she | may deduct | is taxed on | £ |

(b) **Choose the correct option and insert the numerical value.**

If Jen's employer pays her 50p per mile, she | may deduct | is taxed on | £ |

5.1.6 Entertaining customers

If an employee spends money entertaining customers or clients and claims reimbursement, the normal rules seen above will apply.

Rather than reimbursing specific expenses, an employer may simply give an employee an annual allowance to cover expenses. As this is effectively additional salary, it is taxable but the employee may claim a deduction for expenses actually incurred.

The exception to this is an employee may not claim a deduction against a round sum allowance for entertaining costs.

This is because the employer is claiming a deduction against their profits for paying the employee the allowance. Normally, a business cannot claim a deduction for entertaining costs. If the employee is allowed to escape taxation on this part of the allowance, then effectively customers are being entertained with no tax consequences for the employer or employee.

5.2 Contributing to a pension

An employee may save tax by paying into a pension.

5.2.1 Maximum contributions

> **Formula to learn**
>
> The maximum tax relief available for pension contributions each year is the higher of
> * £3,600
> * Earnings for the year

Additional contributions are permitted but no tax relief will be available on these.

5.2.2 Tax relief

Effectively the taxpayer's income is being reduced by the payment into the pension scheme so they are no longer paying tax on the top level of their income. They therefore save the tax they would have paid on this income. This saving may be at 20%, 40% or 45% depending on their level of income. A 20% taxpayer saves tax of 20p for every £1.00 contribution, a 40% taxpayer saves tax at 40p for every £1.00, while a 45% taxpayer would save 45p for every £1.00.

The method of relief is different depending on the type of pension scheme.

Key term

Personal pension scheme	A personal pension scheme is organised by the taxpayer. Contributions are made net of basic rate tax (20%). Additional relief is available for higher and additional rate taxpayers by **extending the basic rate band**. This is identical to the way taxpayers get relief for Gift Aid payments and we will consider this in detail in Chapter 6 – Calculation of income tax.
Occupational scheme	An occupational scheme is one provided by an employer. Contributions are deducted directly from earnings. PAYE is then applied to just the remaining income. This is called a **net pay arrangement**.

5.2.3 Employer contributions

An employer may also contribute to either an occupational scheme or a personal scheme on behalf of the employee.

Employer contributions are not taxable benefits on the employee.

There is no limit on the amount of contributions an employer can make.

5.3 Donations to charity

Employees may request that their employer pays some of their salary to an approved charity of their choice.

The donation is deducted from gross salary before PAYE is applied. It therefore saves the taxpayer tax at their highest marginal rate of tax.

This is sometimes called **'Give-As-You-Earn'** or **GAYE**.

Illustration 11: Income tax return for employed taxpayers

In the exam, you may have to complete pages from the income tax return. A sample page is included below using the data from Activity 2: Car and fuel benefit.

HM Revenue & Customs

Employment
Tax year 6 April 2016 to 5 April 2017 (2016–17)

Your name
Damon

Your Unique Taxpayer Reference (UTR)

Complete an 'Employment' page for each employment or directorship

1 Pay from this employment – the total from your P45 or P60 – before tax was taken off
£ 50000 . 00

2 UK tax taken off pay in box 1
£ – 21000 . 00

3 Tips and other payments not on your P60 – read the 'Employment notes'
£ . 00

4 PAYE tax reference of your employer (on your P45/P60)
/

5 Your employer's name
Stuart Ltd

6 If you were a company director, put 'X' in the box

6.1 If you ceased being a director before 6 April 2016, put the date the directorship ceased in the box DD MM YYYY

7 And, if the company was a close company, put 'X' in the box

8 If you are a part-time teacher in England or Wales and are on the Repayment of Teachers' Loans Scheme for this employment, put 'X' in the box

Benefits from your employment – use your form P11D (or equivalent information)

9 Company cars and vans – the total 'cash equivalent' amount
£ 17070 . 00

10 Fuel for company cars and vans – the total 'cash equivalent' amount
£ 6660 . 00

11 Private medical and dental insurance – the total 'cash equivalent' amount
£ . 00

12 Vouchers, credit cards and excess mileage allowance
£ . 00

13 Goods and other assets provided by your employer – the total value or amount
£ . 00

14 Accommodation provided by your employer – the total value or amount
£ . 00

15 Other benefits (including interest-free and low interest loans) – the total 'cash equivalent' amount
£ . 00

16 Expenses payments received and balancing charges
£ . 00

Employment expenses

17 Business travel and subsistence expenses
£ . 00

18 Fixed deductions for expenses
£ . 00

19 Professional fees and subscriptions
£ . 00

20 Other expenses and capital allowances
£ . 00

ⓘ Share schemes, employment lump sums, compensation, deductions and Seafarers' Earnings Deduction are on the 'Additional information' pages.

SA102 2016   Page E 1   HMRC 12/15

(Adapted from HMRC, 2016)

Chapter summary

- It is important to distinguish between income from employment and self-employment. The basic question is whether the person is employed under a contract of service, or performs services under a contract for services.

- An employee's earnings comprise wages or salary and bonuses and benefits.

- Money earnings are received on the earlier of the time payment is made and when the employee becomes entitled to payment. There are special rules for directors.

- The taxable benefit on a car is a percentage of the car's list price. This varies with carbon dioxide emissions. There is an additional benefit if fuel is provided.

- The private use of a pool car is an exempt benefit.

- There is a taxable benefit for private use of a van (but home to work travel is not treated as private use) plus a further benefit if private fuel is provided.

- If the employer provides the employee with assets for private use, there is a taxable benefit each year of 20% of the value of the assets when first provided.

- Employer loans written off give rise to a taxable benefit. For loans there is a benefit equal to the excess of official rate of interest over interest actually charged.

- The living accommodation benefit is based on the annual value of the property. An additional benefit arises where the cost of the property exceeds £75,000.

- Expenses incurred by the employer in connection with the provision of living accommodation are fully assessable on the employee, unless the employee is in job-related accommodation in which case the benefit is restricted.

- There are certain exempt benefits which are not taxable on employees.

- A deduction is given to employees for using their own vehicle for business travel if any mileage allowance paid is less than the statutory rates. Any excess is taxable.

- Employees are generally allowed a deduction for travel costs incurred in the performance of their duties, or incurred in travelling to and from home to a temporary workplace. Temporary is taken to be not exceeding 24 months.

- Occupational pension schemes are employer-run schemes. No taxable benefit arises in respect of employer contributions made to pension schemes.

- Employee contributions to an occupational pension scheme are deducted from the employee's taxable earnings before tax is applied.

- Individuals can make pension contributions up to the higher of:
  - The basic limit (£3,600 – 2015/16)
  - Earnings

- Employees can make charitable donations under an employer's payroll deduction scheme. Such payments are deductible in arriving at taxable earnings.

- For other employment-related expenses to be deductible, such expenses must be 'wholly, exclusively and necessarily' incurred 'in the performance of' the employee's duties (HMRC, 2014).

Keywords

- **Approved mileage allowance payments scheme:** lays down authorised mileage rates (AMR) at which employees may claim an allowance for business journeys made in their own car

- **Job-related accommodation:** accommodation that is either necessary for the proper performance of duties, or for the better performance of the employee's duties and is customarily provided in that type of employment, or is provided as part of special security arrangements

- **Net pay arrangements:** where an employer deducts an employee's occupational pension contributions from the employee's earnings before they deduct income tax

- **Payroll deduction scheme:** set up by an employer to enable employees to make tax-deductible donations to charity

- **Temporary workplace:** one at which the employee expects to be for no more than 24 months

Activity 1: Basis of assessment

(a) £ | 30,916 |

(b) £ | 3,000 |

Workings

	£
Salary:	
6 April 2016 to 31 October 2016 – $\frac{7}{12}$ × 28,000	16,333
1 November 2016 to 5 April 2017 – $\frac{5}{12}$ × 35,000	14,583
Total salary	30,916
Bonus received between 6 April 2016 and 5 April 2017	3,000

Activity 2: Car and fuel benefit

(a) £ | 23,730 |

Workings

	£
List price + accessories (60,000 + 900)	60,900
30%(W) × £60,900	18,270
Less employee contributions (12 × £100)	(1,200)
Car benefit	17,070
Plus fuel benefit (£22,200 × 30%)	6,660
Total benefit	23,730

(W)	Round down to 165	
	Relevant emissions percentage:	
	165 – 95 =	70
	Divide by 5 =	14
	Add basic	16
		30%

(b) £ | 17,798 |

Workings (not provided in the CBT)

	£
$30\% \times £60,900 \times \dfrac{9}{12}$	13,703
Less employee contributions (9 × £100)	(900)
Car benefit	12,803
Add fuel benefit ($£22,200 \times 30\% \times \dfrac{9}{12}$)	4,995
Total benefit	17,798
Alternatively – $23,730 \times \dfrac{9}{12}$	17,798

Activity 3: Use and gift of employer's asset

In 2016/17, his benefit for the use of the asset is £ | 150 |

In 2016/17, his benefit on the gift of the asset is £ | 550 |

Workings

Use of employer's assets

	£	£
2014/15 Use: 20% × 1,000 × $\frac{6}{12}$	100	
2015/16 Use: 20% × 1,000	200	
2016/17 Use: 20% × 1,000 × $\frac{9}{12}$	150	
		450

Gift

	£	£
2016/17 Higher of:		
• Value when given	500	
• Value when first made available for use less already		
Assessed (1,000 – 450)	550	
le		550

Activity 4: Beneficial loan

The benefit calculated under the average method is £ [350]

The benefit calculated under the strict method is £ [450]

The taxpayer would be taxed on £ [350]

Workings

Average method	£
3% × $\frac{30,000 + 10,000}{2}$	600
Less interest paid	(250)
Benefit	350

Alternative method (strict method)	£
£30,000 × $\frac{8}{12}$ (6 April – 6 December) × 3%	600
£10,000 × $\frac{4}{12}$ (7 December – 5 April) × 3%	100
	700
Less interest paid	(250)
Benefit	450

The taxpayer would not opt for the strict method.

HMRC may opt for the alternative method if it suspects tax avoidance.

Activity 5: Accommodation benefit

(a) £ [nil]

(b) £ [3,500]

(c) £ [7,250]

Workings

Accommodation (house bought in 1999)	£
Annual value	3,000
Less rent paid	(2,500)
	500
Add: 3% × (175,000 – 75,000)	3,000
Taxable benefit	3,500

The property was less than six years old when Ralph moved in so the benefit is based on cost.

Accommodation (house bought in 1992)	£
Annual value	3,000
Less rent paid	(2,500)
	500
Add: 3% × (300,000 – 75,000)	6,750
Taxable benefit	7,250

The property was more than six years old when Ralph moved in so the benefit is based on market value.

Activity 6: Accommodation living expenses

If the property is 'job related' her benefit is £ [900]

If the property is not 'job related' her benefit is £ [1,800]

Workings

Living expenses	£
Lower of:	
(a) Living expenses	1,800
(b) 10% of net earnings:	
= 10% (7,000 + 2,000)	900
Taxable benefit	= 900

Activity 7: Statutory mileage

Jen drives 15,000 miles in the tax year.

(a)   If Jen's employer pays her 30p per mile she

may deduct	£1,250

Workings

Mileage calculation			£
Receives	15,000 × 0.30		4,500
Approved HMRC rates	10,000 × 0.45	4,500	
	5,000 × 0.25	1,250	(5,750)
Deductible			(1,250)

(b)   If Jen's employer pays her 50p per mile she

is taxed on	£1,750

Workings

Mileage calculation		£
Receives	15,000 × 0.50	7,500
Approved HMRC rates	(as above)	(5,750)
Taxable		1,750

Test your learning

1   **Fill in the missing words.**

Someone is regarded as self-employed if they have a contract ⬚ , whereas if they have a contract ⬚ , they will be regarded as an employee.

2   **Fill in the missing words.**

Expenses are allowable if they are incurred ⬚ , ⬚ and ⬚ in the performance of the duties of employment.

3   Brian uses his own car to travel 8,000 business miles in 2016/17. Brian's employer reimburses him with 35p per mile travelled. The approved mileage rate for the first 10,000 business miles travelled is 45p per mile.

The amounts that are taxable/(deductible) in calculating employment income are (both minus signs and brackets can be used to indicate negative numbers):

£ ⬚

4   An employee is provided with a flat by his employer (not job-related accommodation). The annual value of the flat is £4,000; rent paid by the employer amounts to £5,900 per annum.

The taxable value of this benefit for 2016/17 is:

£ ⬚

5   A taxable fuel benefit is reduced by any reimbursement by the employee of the cost of fuel provided for private mileage.

Tick ONE box.

	✓
True	
False	

6   A video recorder costing £500 was made available to Gordon by his employer on 6 April 2015. On 6 April 2016, Gordon bought the recorder for £150, when its market value was £325.

The assessable benefit that arises in 2016/17 is:

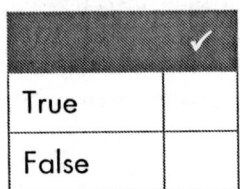

	✓
£325	
£400	
£175	
£250	

7   There is no benefit on the first £10,000 of an interest-free loan.

Tick ONE box.

	✓
True	
False	

8   Gautown was supplied with a petrol engine car by his employer throughout 2016/17. The list price of the car was £24,000 and its CO_2 emissions were 153 g/km.

The taxable benefit arising in respect of the car is:

£ ☐

9   Buster is the Managing Director of Buster Braces Ltd and is supplied with a Bentley (3 litre, petrol engine) which cost £72,000. It has CO_2 emissions of 165 g/km. All running costs are borne by the company. Buster is also provided with a mobile phone for private and business use. The cost of provision of the phone to Buster Braces Ltd is £750 in 2016/17.

The total taxable benefits are:

£ ☐

10 **For each of the following benefits, tick whether they would be taxable or exempt if received by an employee in 2016/17:**

Item	Taxable	Exempt
Write off loan of £8,000 (only loan provided)	☐	☐
Payments by employer of £500 per month into registered pension scheme	☐	☐
Provision of one mobile phone	☐	☐
Provision of a company car for both business and private use	☐	☐
Removal costs of £5,000 paid to an employee relocating to another branch	☐	☐
Accommodation provided to enable the employee to spend longer time in the office	☐	☐

Property income

4

Learning outcomes

1.9K	Identify the main legislative features relating to property income from furnished and unfurnished rented property, rent a room scheme, holiday lets and buy-to-let investments
2.3S	Prepare schedules of income from land and property determining profits and losses
3.2S	Apply deductions and reliefs and claim loss set-offs
3.6S	Describe types of relief which are available on property income including allowable expenses, replacement furniture relief, loss relief – and the circumstances in which each apply

Assessment context

Task 3 in the CBT will test the detailed rules on property income for 10 marks. In addition to this, you may need to explain property rules in the written Task 7 for 10 marks or you may have to complete the property income tax return in Task 8 for 7 marks.

Qualification context

You will not see these areas again in your AAT qualification outside of this unit.

Business context

Property may be an additional source of income for some people. For others, it will be their livelihood. Anyone investing in property needs to understand the tax implications.

Chapter overview

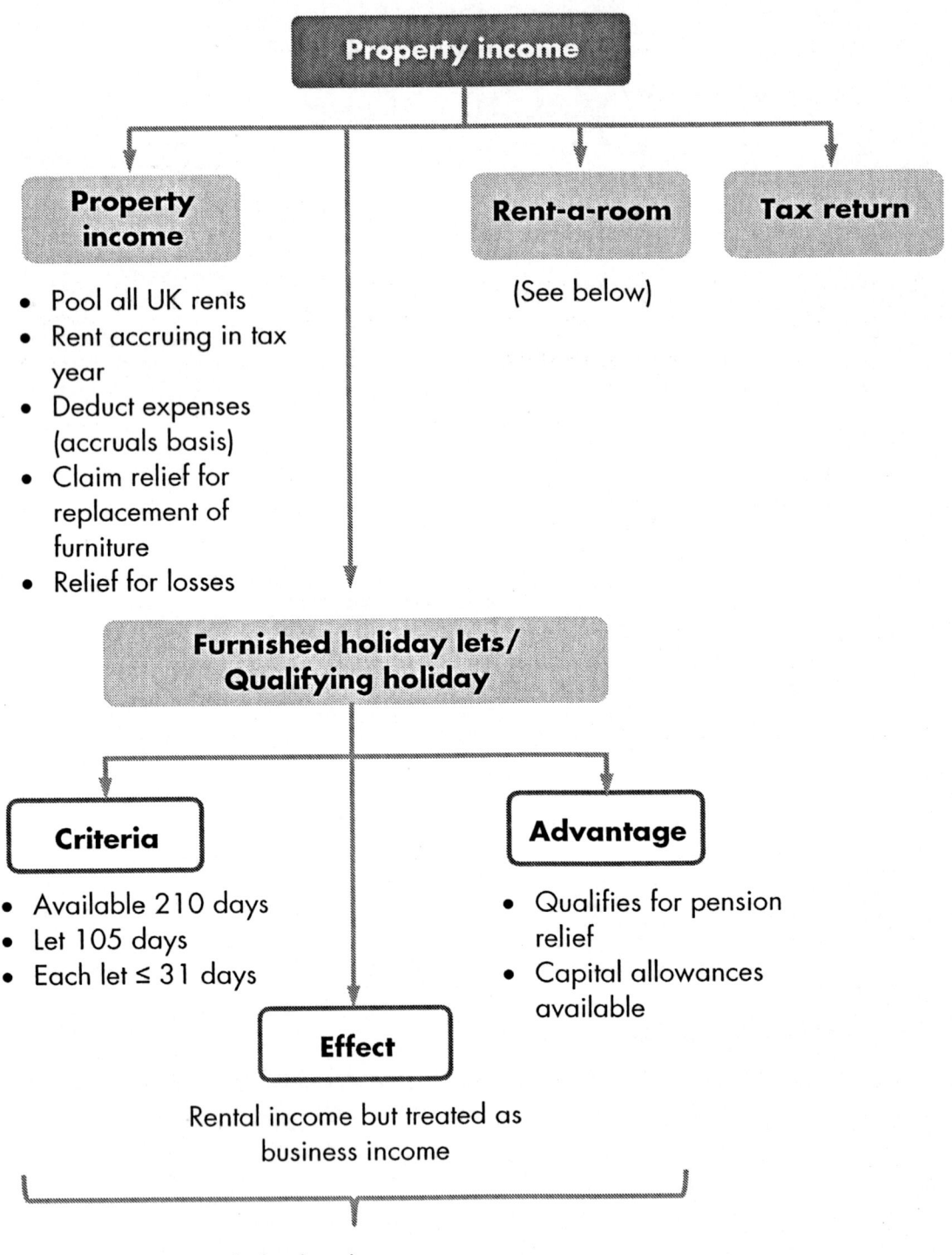

Property income

Property income
- Pool all UK rents
- Rent accruing in tax year
- Deduct expenses (accruals basis)
- Claim relief for replacement of furniture
- Relief for losses

Rent-a-room

(See below)

Tax return

Furnished holiday lets/ Qualifying holiday

Criteria
- Available 210 days
- Let 105 days
- Each let ≤ 31 days

Advantage
- Qualifies for pension relief
- Capital allowances available

Effect

Rental income but treated as business income

Include details in tax return

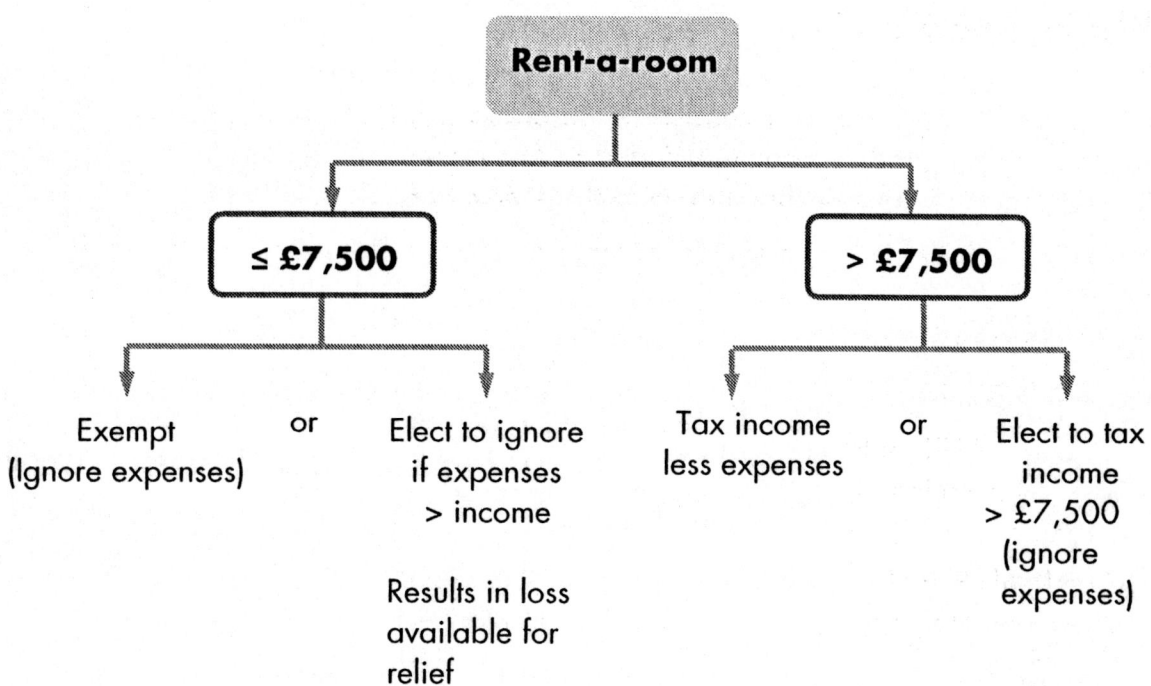

Introduction

Before we can calculate income tax payable for the tax year we need to calculate a taxpayer's total income. This consists of the grand total of their income from various sources. One source of income included in this total would be the income realised from letting out property. This chapter looks at how we calculate this income.

1 Property income

1.1 What is property income?

Property income is all income derived from renting out land and/or buildings.

Key term

Landlord	The person letting out the property
Tenant	The person letting the property
Furnished letting	A property furnished by the landlord
Unfurnished letting	A property in which furniture is provided by the tenant

Note. The tax rules are different for furnished and unfurnished.

1.2 Basis of assessment

A landlord is assessed on rent accruing in the current tax year from UK properties. This is taxed as non-savings income.

Illustration 1: Accruing rent

Susi bought a property on 6 September 2016. She began letting the property immediately for an annual rent of £36,000 payable in advance in 3-monthly instalments due on 6 September, 6 December, 6 March and 6 June.

Rental income is taxed on an accruals basis. This means the income which arises from the letting for the period between 6 September 2016 and 5 April 2017 is taxed in 2016/17. Susi is therefore taxed on £36,000 × 7/12 = £21,000. She actually receives instalments of £9,000 on 6 September, 6 December and 6 March in the tax year, giving total receipts of £27,000, but this is not relevant for the tax calculation.

Activity 1: Accruing rent

Len owns a flat in Lancing. He lets it out unfurnished at an annual rental of £6,000 from 1 January 2016. Rent is payable quarterly in advance. On 1 January 2017, he raised the rent to £6,600 p.a.

Required

Calculate the property income for tax year 2016/17.

£ [   ]

1.3 Allowable deductions from property income

The landlord may deduct all incidental expenses, also calculated on an **accruals basis**. These must be revenue in nature, this means regular ongoing costs giving a short-term benefit, for example insurance. Capital costs are not deductible; these are one-off expenses that give a long-term benefit, for example installing central heating.

The following costs would be allowable if paid by the landlord:

* Advertising, accountancy and insurance
* Business rates and council tax
* Bad debts
* Management and agent's fees

If the landlord borrowed money to purchase the property, the interest paid on the loan is deductible as an expense against property income. Note though the actual repayments of the loan cannot be deducted.

1.4 Repair expenditure

Sometimes it is difficult to distinguish between revenue and capital expenses. A good example would be repair costs. If the costs constitute regular costs required to maintain the property in its current condition then these would be allowable, for example decorating and routine maintenance.

If the repair represents an improvement then it is not allowable, for example if the landlord installed a second bathroom in the property. Note also that if the building is bought in a dilapidated state then the initial costs incurred to make it usable again would also be capital and not allowed.

1.5 Furniture

There is no relief available when the landlord first buys furniture and equipment for the property.

When these assets are replaced the landlord may claim the full cost of the replacement in the tax year in which the replacements were bought.

The following assets would qualify for replacement furniture relief:

* Movable furniture or furnishings, such as beds or suites
* Televisions
* Fridges and freezers
* Carpets and floor coverings
* Curtains
* Linen
* Crockery or cutlery
* Beds and other furniture

If an asset is replaced with a better asset then only the cost of a similar replacement would be allowable.

Note that replacement of integral features such as bathrooms and central heating systems would be covered by the repair rules above.

1.6 Capital allowances

Capital allowances may be claimed on plant and machinery used in the letting business (you would be given a figure for this).

Illustration 2: Allowable expenses

Nadine has let a furnished property for many years. The accrued rent for 2016/17 is £41,000.

Expenses relating to the letting were:

	£
Insurance (year to 31 December 2016)	600
Insurance (year to 31 December 2017)	800

In June 2016, the tenant accidentally flooded the bathroom. Nadine took the opportunity to strip out the aged bathroom suite and convert the bathroom into a wet room at a total cost of £5,000. This included £900 that was the cost of repairing the flood damage.

During the year the washing machine broke and Nadine bought a replacement washer/drier for £400. An equivalent washing machine would have cost £300.

Nadine's property income for 2016/17 is:

	£	£
Rental income		41,000
Less insurance (£600 × 9/12) + (£800 × 3/12)	650	
Replacement furniture relief at cost	300	
Repairs	900	
		(1,850)
Taxable property income		39,150

Note. The rental income and expenses must be dealt with on an accruals basis.

The cost of the flood repairs is allowable because it is a revenue expense. However, the cost of converting the bathroom into a wet room is not allowable because this is a capital expense.

1.7 More than one property – pooling income and expenses

Income and expenses from different properties are pooled to give a single total for property income.

	£
Total property income	X
Total allowable deductions	(X)
Profit/(loss)	X/(X)

Profits and losses on different properties are thus automatically offset.

Illustration 3: Property pooling calculation

Bahrat lets two properties in 2016/17.

Property 1 was bought in June 2016 and let unfurnished from 1 July 2016 at an annual rent of £18,000 per annum. Buildings insurance of £8,000 was paid for the year to 30 June 2017. £1,200 was spent in June 2016 on advertising for tenants.

Property 2 became vacant on 5 April 2016. Bahrat then spent £7,000 on repairing the leaking roof in the property. The unfurnished property was let again with effect from 1 March 2017 for £24,000 per annum, payable monthly in advance. Buildings insurance of £1,800 was incurred for the year to 31 March 2017.

Bahrat's property income for 2016/17 is:

	£	£
Rental income – Property 1		
(9/12 × £18,000)		13,500
Rental income – Property 2		
(1/12 × £24,000)		2,000
Less: Buildings insurance		
– Property 1 (9/12 × £8,000)	6,000	
– Property 2	1,800	
Advertising for tenants	1,200	
Repairs	7,000	
		(16,000)
Overall property loss		(500)

Pooling income and expenses on all let properties effectively allows a loss on one property to be set against income from other properties.

1.8 Losses

If the overall result is a profit it is taxable in the current year.

If the overall result is a loss carry it forward to use against property income in the future. The loss can carry forward indefinitely until it is used.

Activity 2: Property income

Fiona owns a property that she lets furnished on a short-term basis. In the year ended 5 April 2017, she accrued rents of £8,400 and incurred the following expenses:

	£
Agent's commission	360
Mortgage repayments (including interest of £500)	800
Insurance – year to 31 December 2016	400
– year to 31 December 2017	500
Repairs	1,200

Repairs include £300 to replace a broken window; the balance was to install a brand new window. There had been no window here before but Fiona decided the new window would offer views that would encourage future lettings.

She also replaced a single bed with a double bed. The double bed cost £400. An equivalent single bed would have cost £300.

Fiona has a property loss brought forward of £500.

Required

How much is assessable on her as property income in 2016/17?

£ [   ]

---

2 Furnished holiday lets

Key term

Furnished holiday let	A furnished holiday let is a specific type of property that gives certain tax advantages to the landlord.
	This can also be known as qualifying holiday accommodation.

Accommodation counts as a furnished holiday let (FHL) if it is:

(a)   Situated in the UK or in the European Economic Area

(b)   Furnished

(c)   Available for commercial letting to the public for not less than 210 days each tax year

(d)   Actually let for at least 105 days in each tax year

(e)   Holiday tenants should not stay for a period of more than 31 days; however, the property can be let to the same tenant for periods longer than this, provided these long lets do not take up more than 155 days per tax year

FHL accommodation income is taxable as property income but it is treated as a business.

Keep details of income and expenses separate to other properties.

The advantages of having an FHL are that:

(a)   The income may be put in a pension scheme and tax relief claimed. Effectively no tax is paid on income placed in a pension scheme. No tax relief is available from normal rental income.

(b)   Capital allowances are claimed on furniture rather than the renewals basis. This is usually more beneficial.

All UK FHL income is treated as a single business separate to other rental income.

Net losses from a UK FHL business may only be carried forward and offset against future UK FHL income; they cannot be offset against normal property income. Therefore it is important to keep details of income and expenses separate to other properties.

Overseas losses may only be offset against overseas income.

3 Rent-a-room relief

Key term

| **Rent-a-room relief** | This is available when an individual lets out a furnished room or rooms in their main residence. The residence can be owned by the individual or rented from another landlord. |

If gross rent before expenses is £7,500 or less, it is exempt from income tax. This includes charges for services such as laundry. The relief is halved if two people share the income. No relief is available for expenses.

Assessment focus point

The limit is not given in the tax tables in the CBT.

If the income is less than £7,500 and would have resulted in a loss, it is possible to elect not to use the relief.

- Expenses may then be claimed and a loss is available to relieve against other property income.

- The election must be made by 31 January, 22 months from the end of the tax year.

- The election only applies for that year, although a separate claim may be made for other years.

If gross rent is greater than the limit then income will be calculated the normal way (income less expenses) ignoring the relief. However, the taxpayer has the option of choosing to claim the relief. If he does make the claim:

- He will be taxed on the excess over £7,500 with no relief for expenses.

- The election must be made by 31 January, 22 months from the end of the tax year. The election remains in force until it is withdrawn or until rents are less than the limit.

For 2016/17 the deadline for either of the above claims is therefore 31 January 2019.

Illustration 4: Rent-a-room relief

Sylvia owns a flat in London. She has a spare bedroom and during 2016/17 this was let to a chef working at a nearby restaurant for £155 per week, which includes the cost of heating, lighting etc. Sylvia estimates that the extra expenses of these amount to £125 per year. Sylvia provides a television but this had to be replaced in the year at a cost of £200.

Gross rents are £8,060 (52 weeks at £155 per week) which exceeds £7,500.

Sylvia has a choice:

(1) She can be taxed on her actual profit:

	£
Rental income	8,060
Less expenses	(125)
Less replacement of television	(200)
Taxable property income	7,735

(2) She can elect for rent-a-room relief (the alternative basis): total rental income is £8,060 which exceeds the £7,500 limit so taxable property income is £560 (ie £8,060 – £7,500).

Sylvia should elect to use the rent-a-room basis as this will give her a lower amount of taxable property income.

Activity 3: Rent-a-room relief

In 2016/17 Michelle and Michael jointly let out a room in their house to Peter. Peter pays rent of £750 a month. The expenses relating to the let are £1,000.

Required

(a) **What is Michelle's property income, assuming she takes no action?**

£ [   ]

(b) **What is Michelle's property income if she makes an optional election for rent-a-room relief to apply?**

£ [   ]

(c) **When must the election be made?**

[▼]

Picklist:

31 January 2018
5 April 2018
31 January 2019
5 April 2019

(d) **The election must be renewed each year. True or false?**

	✓
True	
False	

4 Land and property section of the income tax return

A sample of the supplementary page to the income tax return form that needs to be completed by taxpayers with property income is included on the following page. This includes the figures from Activity 2: Property income for illustration purposes.

Property income

Do not include furnished holiday lettings, Real Estate Investment Trust or Property Authorised Investment Funds dividends/distributions here.

20 Total rents and other income from property

£ 8 4 0 0 · 0 0

21 Tax taken off any income in box 20 - read the notes

£ · 0 0

22 Premiums for the grant of a lease - from box E on the Working Sheet - read the notes

£ · 0 0

23 Reverse premiums and inducements

£ · 0 0

Property expenses

24 Rent, rates, insurance, ground rents etc.

£ 4 2 5 · 0 0

25 Property repairs and maintenance

£ 3 0 0 · 0 0

26 Loan interest and other financial costs

£ 5 0 0 · 0 0

27 Legal, management and other professional fees

£ 3 6 0 · 0 0

28 Costs of services provided, including wages

£ · 0 0

29 Other allowable property expenses

£ · 0 0

Calculating your taxable profit or loss

30 Private use adjustment - read the notes

£ · 0 0

31 Balancing charges - read the notes

£ · 0 0

32 Annual Investment Allowance

£ · 0 0

33 Business Premises Renovation Allowance (Assisted Areas only) - read the notes

£ · 0 0

34 All other capital allowances

£ · 0 0

Box 35 is not in use

36 Replacement furniture relief - for furnished residential accommodation only - read the notes

£ 3 0 0 · 0 0

37 Rent a Room exempt amount

£ · 0 0

38 Adjusted profit for the year - from box M on the Working Sheet - read the notes

£ 6 5 1 5 · 0 0

39 Loss brought forward used against this year's profits

£ 5 0 0 · 0 0

40 Taxable profit for the year (box 38 minus box 39)

£ 6 0 1 5 · 0 0

41 Adjusted loss for the year - from box M on the Working Sheet - read the notes

£ · 0 0

42 Loss set off against 2015-16 total income - this will be unusual - read the notes

£ · 0 0

43 Loss to carry forward to following year, including unused losses brought forward

£ · 0 0

SA105 2016   Page UKP 2

(Adapted from HMRC, 2016)

Chapter summary

- Property income is all income derived from letting out land and buildings.

- It is calculated on an accruals basis for a tax year and taxed as non-savings income.

- It is net of income and expenditure. Expenditure is allowable if it is for regular ongoing costs, repairs or the replacement of furniture. Capital costs are not allowable.

- Income and expenses on different properties are pooled to give a grand total. A net positive result will be taxable. A net negative result is a loss that may be carried forward and offset against property income in the future.

- Income from qualifying holiday accommodation counts as earnings for pension purposes.

- Capital allowances may be claimed on furniture in qualifying holiday accommodation.

- Rent-a-room relief exempts up to £7,500 of property income when an individual rents out a furnished room or rooms in their main residence.

Keywords

- **Accruals basis:** for taxing rental income means that all rent owing or accruing in a tax year is taxed in that year

- **Furnished holiday lets:** furnished holiday accommodation let on commercial terms for short periods of time each year with a view to realisation of profit

- **Furnished letting:** a letting which includes the use of furniture belonging to the landlord

- **Landlord:** someone who rents out a property to another person

- **Rent-a-room relief:** exempts all or part of the property income arising from an individual renting out part of their main residence

- **Tenant:** the person who occupies the land or building

- **Unfurnished letting:** a letting just of the property without furniture

Activity answers

Activity 1: Accruing rent

Property income £ | 6,150 |

Workings (not provided in the CBT)

	£
Rent (6.4.16 – 31.12.16) $6,000 \times \dfrac{9}{12} =$	4,500
Rent (1.1.17 – 5.4.17) $6,600 \times \dfrac{3}{12} =$	1,650
Total	6,150

Activity 2: Property income

£ | 6,015 |

Workings (not provided in the CBT)

	£
Rents	8,400
Less expenses commission	(360)
Replacement cost of equivalent single bed	(300)
Mortgage interest	(500)
Insurance $(\dfrac{9}{12} \times 400) + (\dfrac{3}{12} \times 500)$	(425)
Repairs to existing window	(300)
Property income	6,515
Less property losses brought forward	(500)
	6,015

Activity 3: Rent-a-room relief

(a) Property income £ | 4,000 |

Workings (not provided in the CBT)

Annual rent is £750 × 12 =	£9,000
Michelle's share is	£4,500
Her exemption is (7,500 / 2)	£3,750
As the rent is above the exemption the relief is ignored and the property income is taxed as normal.	
Michelle's income is ½ (9,000 – 1,000) ie £4,000	

(b) Property income £ | 750 |

Workings (not provided in the CBT)

If Michelle makes the election she claims no relief for her expenses but may claim the rent-a-room exemption.
Michelle's income is ½ (9,000 – 7,500) ie £750

(c) The election must be made by | 31 January 2019 |

The election must be made by 31 January 22 months after the end of the tax year.

(d) | False |

It remains in force until it is withdrawn or until rent falls below the limit.

Test your learning

1 David buys a property for letting on 1 August 2016 and grants a tenancy to Ethel from 1 December 2016 at £3,600 p.a., payable quarterly in advance.

   The rental income taxable in 2016/17 is:

   £

2 John pays buildings insurance premiums for 12 months in advance on 1 October each year to cover all his rental properties. He pays £4,800 in 2015 and £5,200 in 2016.

   What amount for building insurance would be allowed against his rental income for 2016/17?

   £ [   ]

3 **Explain how the loss arising from a furnished holiday let (FHL) can be relieved.**

4 **Where profits are being made, what is the main income tax advantage of letting qualifying holiday accommodation?**

5 Harry owns a property which he lets for the first time on 1 July 2016 at a rent of £4,000 per annum, payable monthly in advance.

   The first tenants left on 28 February 2017 and the property was re-let to new tenants on 4 April 2017 at a rent of £5,000 per annum, payable yearly in advance.

   Harry's allowable expenditure was £1,000 in 2016/17.

   What is his taxable rental income for 2016/17?

   £ [   ]

6 **What is the maximum rental income in a tax year which is exempt from income tax under the rent-a-room scheme?**

   Tick ONE box.

	✓
£3,750	
£4,250	
£7,500	
£10,000	

7 **Which TWO of the following are not advantages of a property being classed as a furnished holiday let?**

	✓
Income can qualify as 'earnings' for pension purposes	
Capital allowances can be claimed on furniture	
Replacement relief can be claimed on furniture	
Losses can be set against other income – not just property income	

Taxable income

5

Learning outcomes

1.2K	Explain the main legislative features relating to income from savings, including exempt savings income
1.8K	Identify the main legislative features relating to dividend income from UK registered companies
2.2S	List non-savings, savings and dividend income checking for completeness
2.5K	Describe taxable and non-taxable savings income
3.1S	Apply allowances that can be set against non-savings income
3.3S	Account for personal allowances

Assessment context

Calculating taxable income is a step on the way to calculating income tax payable. In your CBT, Task 4 will test your understanding of investment income for 6 marks, while Task 5 will assess your knowledge of the computation of total and taxable income for 12 marks. We will go on in the next chapter to build on the information in this chapter and perform the actual tax calculation that will be tested in Task 6 for 10 marks.

Qualification context

If you are studying *Business Tax* as well as *Personal Tax* then the material in this chapter will be useful background for you in your *Business Tax* studies. However, you will not be tested on the material in this chapter in the *Business Tax* CBT.

Business context

Preparation of taxable income computations forms part of the work a tax adviser will perform for their client.

Chapter overview

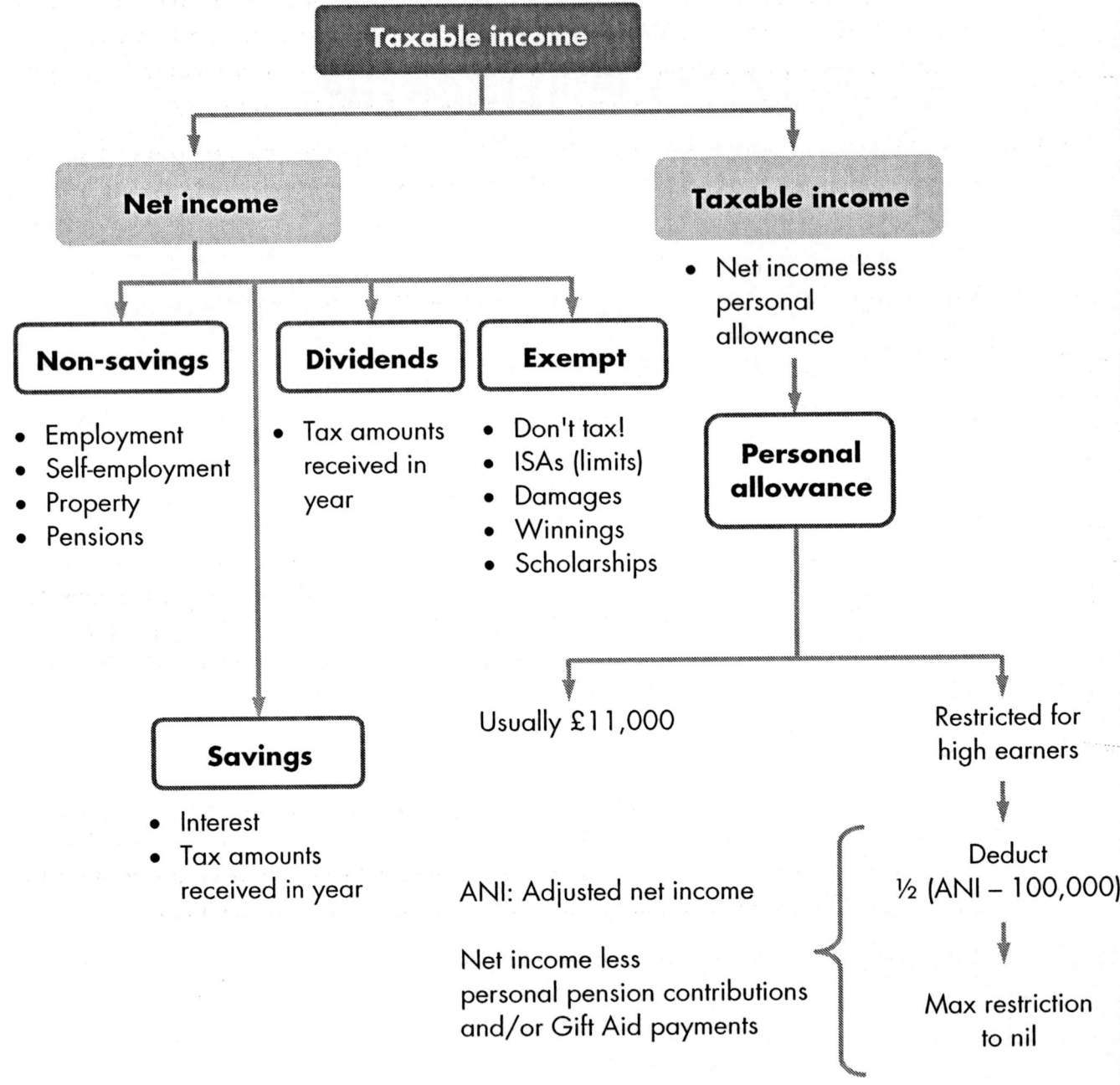

Taxable income

Net income

Taxable income
- Net income less personal allowance

Non-savings
- Employment
- Self-employment
- Property
- Pensions

Dividends
- Tax amounts received in year

Exempt
- Don't tax!
- ISAs (limits)
- Damages
- Winnings
- Scholarships

Personal allowance

Usually £11,000

Restricted for high earners

Deduct ½ (ANI – 100,000)

Max restriction to nil

Savings
- Interest
- Tax amounts received in year

ANI: Adjusted net income

Net income less personal pension contributions and/or Gift Aid payments

Introduction

Having looked at how to calculate **employment income** and **property income** we are now going to look at some additional sources of income, **savings and dividend income**. We'll also identify some **exempt** income that will never be taxed. We are then going to add together all our sources of income to get our **total or net income**, the amount that we will potentially have to pay tax on.

Most taxpayers are given a **personal allowance**, an amount they are allowed to earn before they pay tax. We will deduct this personal allowance from the net income to leave us with our **taxable income**, the amount we will actually pay tax on.

We'll consider the actual calculation of tax in the following chapter.

1 The income tax computation

The **income tax computation** is used to calculate an individual's **income tax liability**.

The income tax liability is the total amount of income tax the taxpayer is due to pay for the tax year.

Key term

Taxable income	To calculate the income tax liability we apply tax rates to **taxable income**. Taxable income is the grand total of a taxpayer's income from all sources after deducting the **personal allowance**, if applicable.
Personal allowance	The personal allowance is the amount of income a taxpayer is allowed to earn before they pay tax. It can be reduced or withdrawn completely for higher earners.

In this chapter we will calculate taxable income. We will then consider how to calculate the income tax liability on the taxable income in the next chapter.

The calculation of taxable income looks like this:

Illustration 1: Proforma income tax computation

	Non-savings income £	Savings income (excluding dividends) £	Dividends £	Total £
Employment income	X			X
Property income	X			X
Interest received		X		X
Dividends from UK companies			X	X
Total/net income	X	X	X	X
Less personal allowance	(X)			(X)
Taxable income	X	X	X	X

Note. Total and net income are actually two different concepts but in your syllabus the terms can be used interchangeably. We will use net income for the rest of the chapter.

You will see there are three columns representing three types of income. We will consider the implications of this in the following section.

Some income will be paid over to the taxpayer **net of tax**, meaning tax has already been deducted at source. An example of this would be a salary payment from an employer. This represents an estimate of the tax the taxpayer is likely to have to pay.

We use the income tax computation to calculate the correct amount of tax that a taxpayer should be paying for the year. We therefore need to include all income **gross** of tax, before these estimated amounts of tax have been deducted.

When the tax liability has been calculated then the individual is allowed to deduct the tax already paid for the tax year. This may or may not be the correct amount.

This could leave the taxpayer having to make an additional tax payment or claim a tax repayment.

2 Non-savings, savings, dividend and exempt income

Different tax rates apply to the three different types of income:

Key term

Non-savings income	This consists of income from employment, self-employment pensions and property income.
Savings income	This consists of interest received in the tax year.
Dividend income	This consists of dividends received in the tax year.

Note that **exempt income** is income that is never charged to income tax.

2.1 Non-savings income

This is all income other than interest and dividends. It includes the following:

- Income from employment (see Chapter 3 Employment income)

- Income from property (see Chapter 4 Property income)

- Income from pensions

- Income from self-employment (the calculation of this income forms part of the *Business Tax* syllabus)

2.2 Savings income

This is interest received. Note it is taxed on an actual basis. If interest is received in the tax year it is taxed. If it is accrued but not received, it is not taxed.

Since 6 April 2016 all interest is received **gross**. There is no longer any requirement for banks and building societies to deduct income tax at source. We simply add together all the interest received in the tax year from all sources and then insert the total into the savings column in the tax computation.

Most taxpayers will not have to pay income tax on interest received unless their interest income is above the **personal savings allowance** (see following chapter).

Illustration 2: Savings income

Gerry receives the following interest:

	£
Lloyds TSB Bank	80
Nationwide Building Society	400
Government interest (gilts)	100

These amounts would be added together to calculate the total interest to be included in the savings column of the tax computation.

	Gross £
Lloyds TSB Bank	80
Nationwide Building Society	400
Government interest (gilts)	100
Total	580

2.3 Dividend income

From 6 April 2016 dividends are received gross. Before this date the dividend used to be received net.

Taxpayers are taxed on the amount of dividend received in a tax year.

Illustration 3: Dividend income

Maria receives a dividend of £900. This is the gross amount that needs to be included in the computation of net income.

Most taxpayers will not have to pay income tax on dividend received unless their dividend income is above the **dividend allowance** (see following chapter).

2.4 Exempt income

Assessment focus point

Certain income is exempt from income tax. Do not include it in your total of taxable income.

If you are typing in an answer and there is exempt income in the question, state that this is exempt or if there is an exempt box to click, make sure you do this – there will be a mark here.

Exempt income includes the following:

2.4.1 Individual savings accounts (ISAs)

(a) These are special savings accounts a taxpayer can invest in.

(b) Individuals may invest up to £15,240 in an individual savings account (ISA) in tax year 2016/17. This could be in the form of cash, shares, unit trusts or insurance policies. Investors may use their entire allowance on one type of investment (eg the whole £15,240 could be invested in cash) or a combination of different investments.

(c) Dividend income from shares and interest income received from cash invested in an ISA are free of income tax. Capital growth is also free of capital gains tax.

(d) An ISA may be opened by someone 16 years old and over if it only contains cash.

(e) ISAs containing investments other than cash may only be opened by someone at least 18 years old.

2.4.2 Others

- Damages awarded as a result of personal injury or death and interest thereon
- Scholarships/grants, if paid to a student; taxable if paid to their parent as part of their employment income
- Prizes, lotto winnings, gambling winnings
- Premium bond prizes

Activity 1: Taxable and exempt income

Foster receives the following income:

	£
Building society interest	40
Dividend from an ISA investment	900
Rent	6,000
Non-ISA dividends	450

Required

Complete the following table.

Use the picklist options to list the sources of income under the appropriate headings (exempt, non-savings, savings or dividend income).

Record the amounts received under the appropriate column heading (exempt, non-savings, savings and dividends).

You do not need to total the columns.

Solution

	Exempt income £	Non-savings income £	Savings income £	Dividend income £
Exempt income				
Non-savings income				
Savings income				
Dividend income				

Picklist options:	
Building society interest	ISA dividend
Rent	Non-ISA dividend

3 Computation of taxable income

We will now revisit the full income tax computation we looked at in Section 1.

3.1 Net income

In a tax year, all income must be brought together and totalled.

The income is split into three columns representing the three types of income subject to tax:

- Non-savings income
- Savings income
- Dividend income

This gives us net income.

3.2 Taxable income

The personal allowance of £11,000 is then usually deducted from the total/net income to give the taxable amount.

The personal allowance is initially available to all taxpayers, including children.

The personal allowance is reduced for taxpayers who have income in excess of £100,000. The allowance can be potentially reduced to nil.

It is usually most beneficial to deduct the personal allowance against non-savings income before savings income then dividend income.

Illustration 4: Taxable income

In 2016/17, Joe has trade profits of £3,000 and receives bank interest of £17,500 and dividends of £500. Joe's taxable income for 2016/17 is:

	Non-savings income £	Savings income £	Dividend Income £	Total £
Trade profits	3,000			3,000
Bank interest		17,500		17,500
Dividends			500	500
Net income	3,000	17,500	500	21,000
Less personal allowance	(3,000)	(8,000)	–	(11,000)
Taxable income	–	9,500	500	10,000

Activity 2: Taxable income

Quentin earns a salary of £3,000 in 2016/17. He receives rental income of £1,000, building society interest of £3,750 and a dividend of £5,000.

Required

Prepare a computation of taxable income for 2016/17, clearly showing the distinction between the different types of income.

Solution

	Non-savings income £	Savings income £	Dividend income £	Total £
Employment income				
Property income				
Building society interest				

	Non-savings income £	Savings income £	Dividend income £	Total £
Dividend income				
Net income				
Less personal allowance				
Taxable income				

4 Restricting the personal allowance

4.1 The basic calculation

If an individual has net income in excess of £100,000 then the personal allowance must be reduced.

It is reduced by £1 for every £2 income the taxpayer has over the £100,000 limit.

The personal allowance may be reduced to £0 if income is greater than or equal to £122,000.

Formula to learn

Restriction = ½ (net income – 100,000) [limit but not formula given in CBT].

Illustration 5: Personal allowance restriction

In 2016/17, Kelvin has gross employment income of £98,000, receives building society interest of £1,500 and dividends of £5,000. Kelvin's net income for 2016/17 is:

	Non-savings income £	Savings income £	Dividend income £	Total £
Net income	98,000	1,500	5,000	104,500

The total is above the adjustment threshold of £100,000 so we must reduce the personal allowance.

	£
Net income	104,500
Less income limit	(100,000)
Excess	4,500
Personal allowance	11,000
Less half excess (4,500/2)	(2,250)
Adjusted personal allowance	8,750

The taxable income is therefore:

	Non-savings income £	Savings income £	Dividend income £	Total £
Net income	98,000	1,500	5,000	104,500
Less personal allowance	(8,750)	–	–	(8,750)
Taxable income	89,250	1,500	5,000	95,750

Activity 3: Personal allowance restriction

Karen has net income of £107,000 (all non-savings income).

Required

What personal allowance does Karen receive for 2016/17?

Solution

Her personal allowance is £ _____

Her taxable income is   £ _____

4.2 Charitable donations/pension payments

If a taxpayer makes Gift Aid or personal pension scheme contributions in the year (see next chapter), then they are allowed to deduct the payments from net income before calculating the restriction on the personal allowance.

Both of these payments are made net by the taxpayer but it is the gross amount that is deducted from the net income. We will consider this in detail in the next chapter.

Total income after deducting Gift Aid and personal pension contributions is called **adjusted net income**.

Note. Gift Aid and personal pension contributions are only deducted from total income for the purpose of calculating the personal allowance; they are not deducted from income in the tax computation.

Illustration 6: Personal allowance restriction with Gift Aid payment

As per Illustration 5 in 2016/17, Kelvin has gross employment income of £98,000 and receives building society interest of £1,500 and dividends of £5,000. However, he now makes a gross payment to charity of £1,000 under Gift Aid. Kelvin's net income for 2016/17 is still:

	Non-savings income £	Savings income £	Dividend income £	Total £
Net income	98,000	1,500	5,000	104,500

The total is above the adjustment threshold of £100,000 so we must reduce the personal allowance. However, as he has made a payment to charity under Gift Aid we are allowed to reduce the net income before calculating the restriction:

	£
Net income	104,500
Less gross Gift Aid payment	(1,000)
Adjusted net income	103,500
Less income limit	(100,000)
Excess	3,500
Personal allowance	11,000
Less half excess (3,500/2)	(1,750)
Adjusted personal allowance	9,250

The taxable income is therefore:

	Non-savings income £	Savings income £	Dividend income £	Total £
Net income	98,000	1,500	5,000	104,500
Less personal allowance	(9,250)	–	–	(9,250)
Taxable income	88,750	1,500	5,000	95,250

Activity 4: Personal allowance with personal pension payment

Karen, who has net income of £107,000, now makes a personal pension payment of £2,000 gross.

Required

What personal allowance will Karen receive? What is her taxable income?

Solution

Her personal allowance is   £ _____

Her taxable income is   £ _____

We will revisit Gift Aid and personal pension payments in the next chapter.

Chapter summary

- There are three types of income in the income tax computation: non-savings, savings and dividend.

- Non-savings income includes employment income, property income, trading (or business) income and pension income.

- Savings income is interest received.

- Dividend income is dividends received.

- Exempt income includes income from individual savings accounts (ISAs) and gambling winnings.

- Tax computations must be prepared for a tax year.

- All the components of an individual's income are added together to arrive at 'net income'.

- Net income less the personal allowance gives 'taxable income'.

- The personal allowance is deducted first from non-savings income, then from savings income and finally from dividend income. It is reduced by £1 for every £2 that the individual's net income exceeds the income limit of £100,000.

- The net income figure for comparison to the income limit for the personal allowance is reduced by gross Gift Aid donations and personal pension contributions.

Keywords

- **Dividend income:** dividends received from a company

- **Net income:** an individual's total income calculated prior to deducting the personal allowance

- **Non-savings income:** income other than interest and dividends

- **Personal allowance:** the amount of income a taxpayer may receive before paying tax

- **Savings income:** interest received, for example from a bank or building society

- **Total income:** technically a different sub-total to net income but in your syllabus the terms may be used interchangeably

- **Taxable income:** an individual's net income minus the personal allowance

Activity 1: Taxable and exempt income

	Exempt income £	Non-savings income £	Savings income £	Dividend income £
Exempt income				
ISA dividend	900			
Non-savings income				
Rent		6,000		
Savings income				
Building society interest			40	
Dividend income				
Non-ISA dividend				450

Activity 2: Taxable income

	Non-savings income £	Savings income £	Dividend income £	Total £
Employment income	3,000			3,000
Property income	1,000			1,000
Building society interest		3,750		3,750
Dividend income			5,000	5,000
Net income	4,000	3,750	5,000	12,750
Less personal allowance	(4,000)	(3,750)	(3,250)	(11,000)
Taxable income	nil	nil	1,750	1,750

Activity 3: Personal allowance restriction

Her personal allowance is | £7,500 |

Her taxable income is | £99,500 |

Workings

	£
Personal allowance	11,000
Less ½ (107,000 – 100,000) =	(3,500)
Adjusted personal allowance	7,500
Net income	107,000
Personal allowance	(7,500)
Taxable income	99,500

Activity 4: Personal allowance with personal pension payment

Her personal allowance is   £8,500

Her taxable income is   £98,500

Workings

	£
Net income	107,000
Less personal pension payment	(2,000)
Adjusted net income	105,000
Personal allowance	11,000
Less ½ (105,000 – 100,000)	(2,500)
Adjusted personal allowance	8,500
Net income	107,000
Personal allowance	(8,500)
Taxable income	98,500

Test your learning

1 **Classify the following types of income by ticking the correct box:**

	Non-savings income	Savings income	Dividend income
Employment income	☐	☐	☐
Dividends	☐	☐	☐
Property income	☐	☐	☐
Bank interest	☐	☐	☐
Pension income	☐	☐	☐
Interest on government stock	☐	☐	☐

2 **Complete the table below to show the amount of income that would be included in a tax return for 2016/17. If your answer is zero, please put a '0'.**

	Amount received £	Amount in tax return £
Building society interest	240	
Interest on an individual savings account	40	
Dividends	160	
Interest from government gilts	350	

3 In 2016/17, Joe has employment income of £30,000 and receives dividends of £300 and premium bond winnings of £500.

Use the table below to show his taxable income for 2016/17.

	Non-savings income £	Dividend income £	Total £

4. Pratish receives property income of £3,000 and building society interest of £9,000 in 2016/17.

   Use the table below to show his taxable income for 2016/17.

	Non-savings income £	Savings income £	Total £

5. Jesse has employment income of £112,200 in 2016/17. He also received building society interest of £5,000, a prize of £50 in an internet competition and dividends of £4,000.

   Use the table below to show Jesse's taxable income for 2016/17.

	Non-savings income £	Savings income £	Dividend income £	Total £

Calculation of income tax

6

Learning outcomes

3.4S	Calculate income tax payable
3.5S	Describe taxation relief which can be given on income from employment including deductible (allowable) expenses, pension's relief and charitable donations

Assessment context

You will have to calculate income tax payable in Task 6 of your assessment for 10 marks.

Qualification context

If you are studying *Business Tax*, then the material in this chapter will be useful background but you will not be tested on these areas outside of this unit.

Business context

Calculating income tax payable is the main task a tax adviser will perform for their client.

Chapter overview

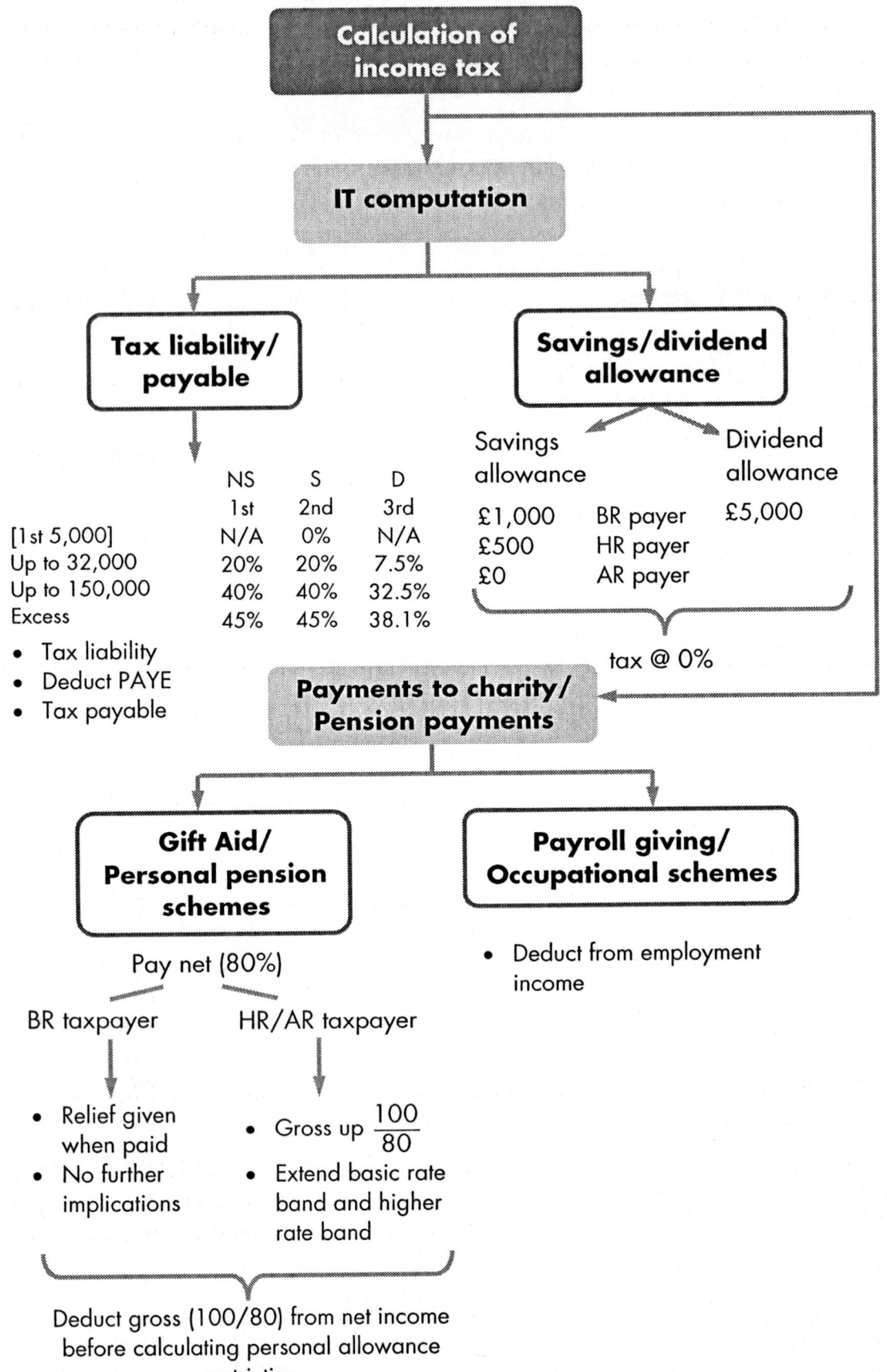

Calculation of income tax

IT computation

Tax liability/ payable

Savings/dividend allowance

	NS	S	D
	1st	2nd	3rd
[1st 5,000]	N/A	0%	N/A
Up to 32,000	20%	20%	7.5%
Up to 150,000	40%	40%	32.5%
Excess	45%	45%	38.1%

- Tax liability
- Deduct PAYE
- Tax payable

Savings allowance

£1,000	BR payer
£500	HR payer
£0	AR payer

Dividend allowance

£5,000

tax @ 0%

Payments to charity/ Pension payments

Gift Aid/ Personal pension schemes

Payroll giving/ Occupational schemes

- Deduct from employment income

Pay net (80%)

BR taxpayer

HR/AR taxpayer

- Relief given when paid
- No further implications

- Gross up $\dfrac{100}{80}$
- Extend basic rate band and higher rate band

Deduct gross (100/80) from net income before calculating personal allowance restriction

Introduction

The calculation of income tax will appear complex at first. There is a set of basic rules but these can be applied in many different combinations depending on a taxpayer's circumstances, meaning there are many different scenarios for you to get to grips with.

In this chapter we will consider some but not all of the possible scenarios. The more examples you study and questions you attempt the more familiar you will become with how the rules operate.

1 Calculation of income tax liability

Income tax is calculated at different rates depending on the type and level of income the taxpayer has.

The various rates for 2016/17 are summarised in the diagram below. This data will be provided for you in the taxation tables in your assessment.

The taxable income we calculated in the previous chapter is taxed in the following order:

(1) Non-savings income
(2) Savings income
(3) Dividend income

So, on the diagram we move from left to right.

Illustration 1: Calculation of tax liability

Taxable income	Non-savings	Savings	Dividends	
	45%	45%	38.1%	} Additional rate
150,000	40%	40%	32.5%	} Higher rate
32,000				
5,000	20%	20%	7.5%	} Basic rate
0		0%		

(Starting rate applies to the band from 0 to 5,000)

Note we have different **tax bands**.

The **starting rate band** covers taxable income from £1 to £5,000 but only applies to savings income.

The basic rate band covers income from £1 to £32,000. Note the starting rate band forms the first £5,000 of the basic rate band. The starting rate only applies to taxpayers who have less than £5,000 taxable non-savings income so in most calculations it will be ignored.

The **higher rate band** covers income from £32,001 to £150,000.

The **additional rate band** covers income over £150,000.

These bands may be adjusted for taxpayers who make payments to charity under Gift Aid or pay into a personal pension scheme.

In addition to these bands, there is a **personal savings allowance** that applies to savings income and a **dividend allowance** that applies to dividend income.

We apply these rates to give us our **income tax liability**.

Key term

> **Income tax liability**   The total amount of tax that should be paid on our income.

Don't forget that an employed taxpayer will have had income tax deducted from their salary before it has been paid to them. This represents an estimated prepayment of income tax for the year. We deduct this from the income tax liability to see whether there is any further **income tax payable** for the year.

It is possible that the taxpayer has paid too much tax. If they have there will be **income tax repayable**.

Key term

> **Income tax payable**   Outstanding income tax due for the tax year.
>
> **Income tax repayable**   Income tax due to the taxpayer because they have overpaid.

> **Assessment focus point**
>
> Read the requirement very carefully to see if you are being asked to calculate **income tax liability** or **income tax payable**. You will lose marks or waste time if you calculate the wrong one.

2 Taxation of non-savings income

Non-savings income is taxed first.

- It is taxed initially in the starting rate/basic rate band at 20%.
- It is then taxed in the higher rate band at 40%.
- Finally it is taxed in the additional rate band at 45%.

> **Illustration 2: Non-saving income**
>
> Nathan has taxable income of £185,000 consisting entirely of non-savings employment income. PAYE of £65,000 has been deducted.
>
> The non-savings income uses all the basic rate band of £32,000, the next £118,000 of income falls into the higher rate band and the excess above that falls into the additional rate band.

The income tax liability is:

	Income tax £
Non-savings income	
32,000 × 20%	6,400
118,000 × 40%	47,200
150,000	
35,000 × 45%	15,750
185,000	
Income tax liability	69,350
Less PAYE	(65,000)
Income tax payable	4,350

This can be illustrated on the diagram as follows:

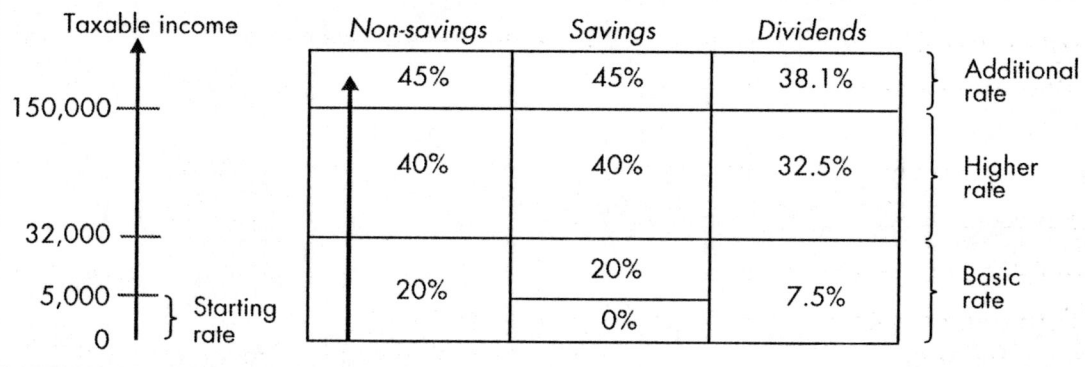

3 Savings income

Once we have taxed non-savings income we then move on to tax savings income.

We begin taxing savings income in the bands at the point where we finished taxing the non-savings income. So in the previous illustration (Illustration 2) Nathan would pay tax on any savings income in the additional rate band as he has already used his basic rate and higher rate band.

Savings income is taxed as follows:

- At 0% on any savings falling in the starting rate band
- At 20% on any savings falling in the basic rate band
- At 40% on any savings falling in the higher rate band
- At 45% on any savings falling in the additional rate band

However, there is a further complication in that taxpayers will potentially receive the **personal savings allowance**. This represents savings income that is taxed at 0%. Taxpayers receive the personal savings allowance as follows:

A basic rate taxpayer (one who has adjusted net income of less than £43,000) receives a personal savings allowance of £1,000.

A higher rate taxpayer (one who has adjusted net income greater than £43,000 but no more than £150,000) receives a personal savings allowance of £500.

An additional rate taxpayer (one who has adjusted net income greater than £150,000) does not receive a personal savings allowance.

(You will note these thresholds represent the relevant bands plus the personal allowance where this is available so for example the basic rate test equals £32,000 plus £11,000 equals £43,000, the higher rate test equals £150,000 plus £0 as no personal allowance would be available for a taxpayer with £150,000 worth of income.)

Illustration 3: Savings income example 1

Sasha has net income of £41,120 (before the personal allowance) and taxable income of £30,120. Of this, £18,920 is non-savings income and £11,200 is savings income.

Her net income is less than £43,001 so she is a basic rate taxpayer. She is therefore entitled to a personal savings allowance of £1,000.

Her non-savings income will use up all of the starting rate band and some of the basic rate band. She will therefore pay income tax on her savings income in excess of the personal savings allowance at 20%.

The income tax liability is:

	Income tax £
Non-savings income	
18,920 × 20%	3,784
Savings income	
1,000 × 0% (personal savings allowance)	0
10,200 × 20% (11,200 – 1,000)	2,040
30,120	
Income tax liability	5,824

This can be illustrated on the diagram as below.

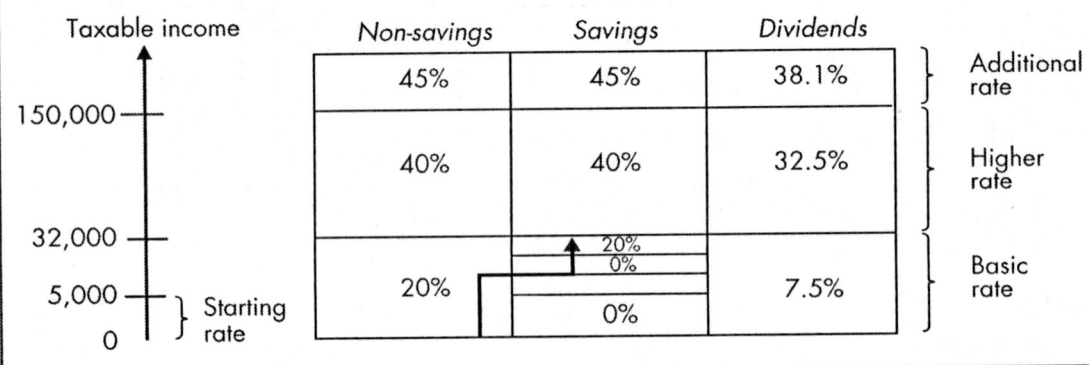

Illustration 4: Savings income example 2

Dave has net income of £90,000 (before the personal allowance) and taxable income of £79,000. Of this, £70,000 is non-savings income and £9,000 is savings income.

His net income is greater than £43,000 but less than £150,000 so he is a higher rate taxpayer. He is therefore entitled to a personal savings allowance of £500.

His non-savings income will use up all of the starting rate band and the basic rate band. He will therefore pay income tax on his savings income in excess of the personal savings allowance at 40%.

The income tax liability is:

	Income tax £
Non-savings income	
32,000 × 20%	6,400
38,000 × 40% (70,000 – 32,000)	15,200
70,000	
Savings income	
500 × 0% (personal savings allowance)	0
8,500 × 40% (9,000 – 500)	3,400
79,000	
Income tax liability	25,000

This can be illustrated on the diagram below.

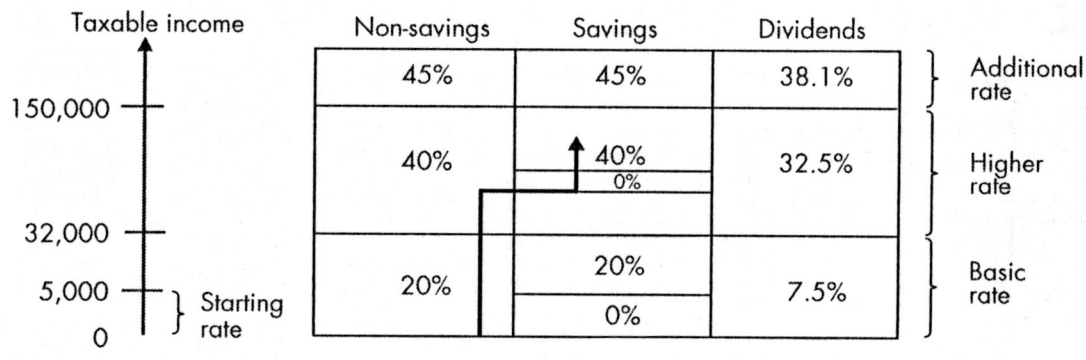

Illustration 5: Savings income example 3

Frank has net income of £180,000. He receives no personal allowance so his taxable income is also £180,000. Of this, £100,000 is non-savings income and £80,000 is savings income.

His net income is greater than £150,000 so he is an additional rate taxpayer. He is therefore not entitled to a personal savings allowance.

His non-savings income will use up all of the starting rate band and the basic rate band. He will therefore pay income tax on his savings income initially at 40% and then 45%.

The income tax liability is:

	Income tax £
Non-savings income	
32,000 × 20%	6,400
68,000 × 40% (100,000 – 32,000)	27,200
100,000	
Savings income	
50,000 × 40%	20,000
150,000	
30,000 × 45% (80,000 – 50,000)	13,500
£180,000	
Income tax liability	67,100

This can be illustrated on the diagram below.

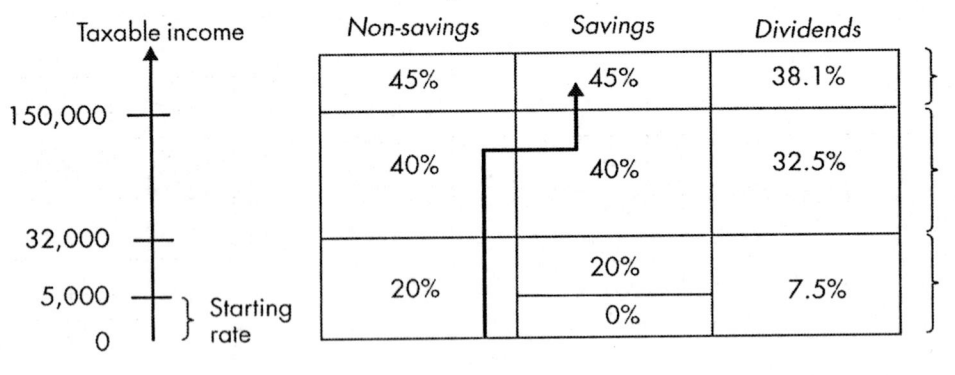

Activity 1: Income tax liability

In 2016/17 Jules, who is single, has employment income of £35,500 and building society interest of £9,000.

Required

Calculate the income tax liability.

Solution

	Non-savings income £	Savings income £	Total £

4 Savings income and the starting rate band

Remember that the order of taxation is:

(1) Non-savings income
(2) Savings income
(3) Dividend income

There is a special rate that applies to taxpayers who have no or low amounts of non-savings income but have savings income.

If any savings income falls within the first £5,000 of taxable income, then it is taxed at a special rate of 0%.

The personal savings allowance would also be available in these circumstances. Note that here it acts in addition to the starting rate band.

Illustration 6: Savings income starting rate

Tamara has net income in 2016/17 of £21,000 giving taxable income of £10,000 following the deduction of the personal allowance. £2,000 is non-savings income and £8,000 is savings income. As her net income is below £43,000 she is entitled to the full personal savings allowance of £1,000.

Her income tax liability is:

	Income tax £
Non-savings income	
2,000 × 20%	400
Savings income	
3,000 × 0%	0
5,000 (starting rate band limit)	
1,000 × 0% (personal savings allowance)	0
4,000 × 20% (8,000 – 3,000 – 1,000)	800
Income tax liability	1,200

This can be illustrated on the diagram below.

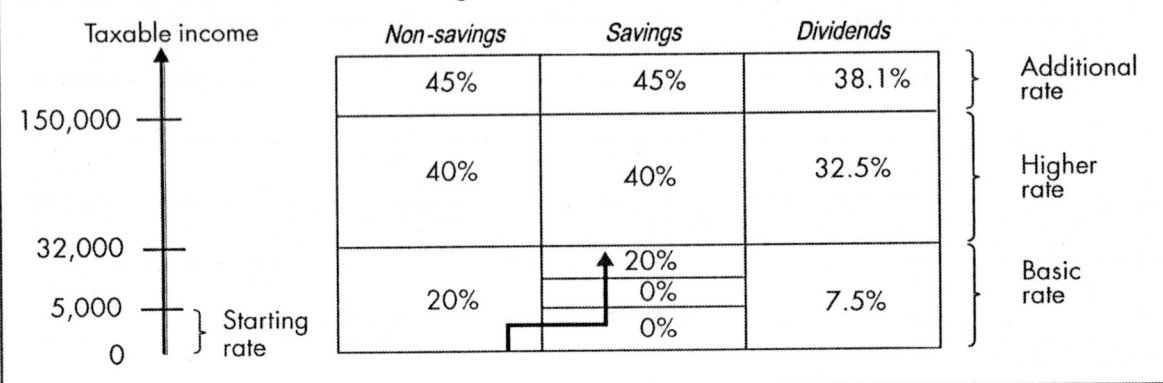

Activity 2: Starting rate band

Tegan earns a salary of £12,000. She receives bank interest of £40,000.

Required

Calculate her income tax liability for 2016/17.

Solution

	Non-savings income £	Savings income £	Total £

5 Dividend income

Once we have taxed non-savings income and savings income, we then move on to tax dividend income.

As before, we begin taxing dividend income in the bands at the point where we finished taxing the savings income.

Dividend income is taxed as follows:

- At 7.5% on any dividend income falling in the basic rate band
- At 32.5% on any dividend income falling in the higher rate band
- At 38.1% on any dividend income falling in the additional rate band

However, there is a further complication in that taxpayers will receive the dividend allowance. This represents dividend income that is taxed at 0%. All taxpayers receive a dividend allowance of £5,000 regardless of their level of net income.

Illustration 7: Dividend income

Douglas has taxable income of £165,000. Of this, £120,000 is non-savings income, £20,000 is savings income and £25,000 is dividend income.

Douglas is clearly an additional rate taxpayer so he will not receive a personal savings allowance. However, he is entitled to the dividend allowance.

The non-savings income of £120,000 uses all the basic rate band of £32,000 and £88,000 of the higher rate band. The £20,000 interest uses a further £20,000 of the higher rate band, leaving a balance of £10,000 remaining. The first £5,000 of dividend income is taxed at 0% because of the dividend allowance but this uses up £5,000 of the remaining higher rate band, leaving £5,000 available for the dividend. The next £5,000 of dividend is therefore taxed in the higher rate band at 32.5%, with the balance of £15,000 taxed at 38.1%.

The income tax liability is:

	Income tax £
Non-savings income	
32,000 × 20%	6,400
88,000 × 40%	35,200
Savings income	
20,000 × 40%	8,000
Dividend income	
5,000 × 0% (dividend allowance)	0
5,000 × 32.5%	1,625
150,000	
15,000 × 38.1% (25,000 – 5,000 – 5,000)	5,715
165,000	
Income tax liability	56,940

This can be illustrated on the diagram below.

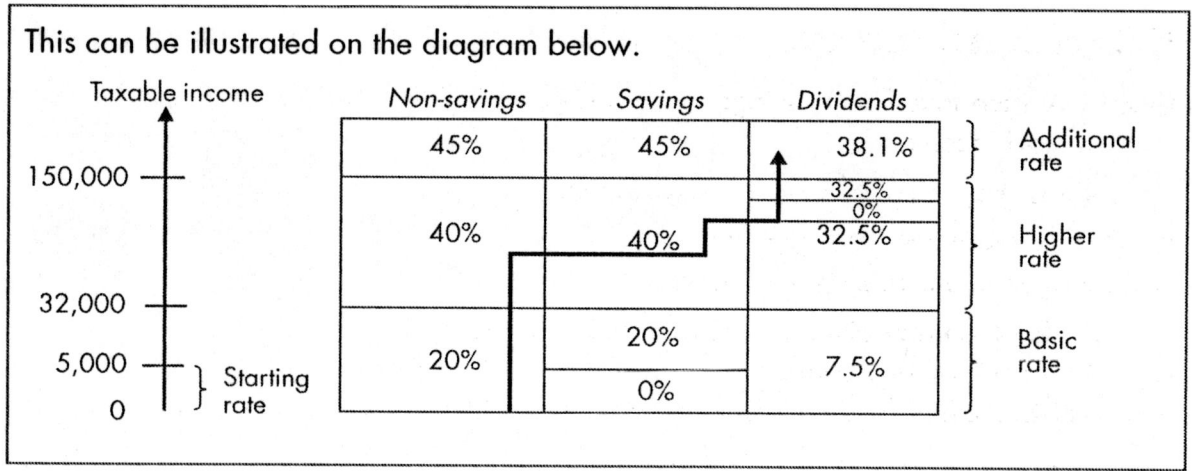

Activity 3: Income tax payable

Arthur has a salary of £125,000 (PAYE £42,000). He received bank interest of £10,000 and dividends of £10,000.

Required

Calculate the net income tax payable for 2016/17.

Solution

	Non-savings income £	Savings income £	Dividend income £	Total £

	Non-savings income £	Savings income £	Dividend income £	Total £

6 Extending the bands

Certain donations to UK registered charities or payments into personal pension schemes are eligible for tax relief.

Essentially, the income the taxpayer puts into the pension scheme/gives to charity is not taxable. The taxpayer therefore saves the tax they would have paid on that income.

Different taxpayers will therefore be entitled to relief at different rates.

Most taxpayers are employees who have already paid their tax via PAYE. By giving money to charity/paying into a pension they are therefore entitled to a refund of tax already paid on this income. Most taxpayers pay tax at 20% so making a payment of £100 would entitle them to a repayment of £20.

It would be onerous for the taxpayer and the Government if everyone who made such a payment had to apply to the Government for a tax refund so to simplify the administration payments are always made **net** of basic rate (20%) tax. The charity/pension will then reclaim the 20% tax from HMRC on behalf of all its donors in one go, saving much time and effort.

The taxpayer has therefore obtained relief at 20% as the charity/pension receives the full 100% but it has only cost the taxpayer 80%. This is effectively the same as the taxpayer giving the charity/pension 100% and then claiming the 20% tax back from the Government that they have already paid on that income.

If the taxpayer does pay tax at 20% then no further action is required on their part.

Higher rate (40%) taxpayers are entitled to an additional 20% (40% – 20%) relief on their gross donation/pension contribution. Additional rate taxpayers are entitled to an additional 25% (45% – 20%) relief on their gross donation/pension contribution.

Additional (20% or 25%) relief is given for charitable donations/pension contributions made by higher/additional rate taxpayers by a process known as 'extending the bands'. This moves income that would have been taxed at a higher rate into a lower rate band, effectively giving the taxpayer a discount on their tax bill.

The basic rate upper limit becomes:

$32,000 + (\text{payments} \times {}^{100}/_{80})$ – income is moved out of higher rate into basic rate saving 20% (40% – 20%)

The higher rate limit becomes:

$150,000 + (\text{payment} \times {}^{100}/_{80})$ – income is moved out of additional rate into higher rate saving a further 5% (45% – 40%). This combined with the basic rate extension above gives the taxpayer a 25% saving (20% + 5%).

Assessment focus point

If a taxpayer makes a payment to charity under Gift Aid or makes a payment into a personal pension scheme, gross up the amount paid by 100/80 and then add this total to the basic rate and higher rate band before calculating the tax liability.

Double check that the figure has not been given to you gross in the question. If it is already gross don't gross it up again.

Illustration 8: Gift Aid donation

Gustav has taxable income (all non-savings) of £50,000 in 2016/17.

Assuming that Gustav does not make any Gift Aid donations or personal pension contributions in 2016/17 his income tax liability will be:

	£
32,000 × 20%	6,400
18,000 × 40%	7,200
50,000	13,600

Now think about the situation where Gustav makes a Gift Aid donation of £8,000 in 2016/17. The Gift Aid donation will have been paid net of 20% tax. This means that the gross amount of the payment is £8,000 × 100/80 = £10,000 and Gustav's basic rate band must be extended by £10,000. His income tax liability is calculated as follows:

	£
32,000 × 20%	6,400
10,000 (extended basic rate band) × 20%	2,000
8,000 × 40%	3,200
50,000	11,600

Extending the basic rate band means that £10,000 more income is taxed at the basic rate and therefore £10,000 less income is taxed at the higher rate. The difference between the tax liabilities with and without the Gift Aid donation is £10,000 × (40 − 20)% = £2,000. The total tax relief is:

	£
Basic rate relief given by net payment (10,000 − 8,000)	2,000
Higher rate relief given by extending basic rate band	2,000
Total tax relief (which equates to 40% of the gross donation)	4,000

Activity 4: Tax liability with Gift Aid donation

In 2016/17, Charlie has employment income of £100,000. He wishes to make a donation of £8,000 (net) to charity.

Required

For 2016/17, calculate Charlie's:

(a) Taxable income

£ [   ]

(b) Tax liability if he does not make the donation

£ [   ]

(c) Tax liability if he does make the donation

£ [   ]

(d) Total tax saved if he does make the donation

£ [   ]

Remember that a personal pension contribution or Gift Aid payment is deducted from total income before restricting the personal allowance. It is the **gross** payment that is deducted (payment $\times {}^{100}/_{80}$).

7 Payroll giving and occupational pension schemes

A taxpayer may also donate to charity via their employer. Under payroll giving, the taxpayer requests that their employer pay some of their salary directly to charity.

A taxpayer may contribute to an occupational pension scheme. This is a pension scheme provided by the employer. Contributions will be deducted directly from the employee's salary.

The taxpayer will obtain tax relief on both of these payments. As they are deducted from salary, they reduce the taxpayer's taxable income and thus their tax liability.

Taxpayers will save at either 20%, 40% or 45% depending on their level of income.

There is no need to extend the basic rate band for these payments.

Chapter summary

- Income is categorised into different types: non-savings, savings and dividend. Each type of income suffers different rates of tax, depending on whether the income falls into the basic or higher rate bands or over the additional rate threshold.

- Non-savings income is taxed first (at 20%, then 40%, then 45%) then savings income (at 0%, then 20%, then 40%, then 45%) and finally dividend income (at 7.5%, then 32.5%, then 38.1%).

- The savings income starting rate of 0% applies to savings income within the savings income starting rate band.

- A personal savings allowance is available at £1,000 for a basic rate taxpayer, £500 for a higher rate taxpayer and £0 for an additional rate taxpayer. Savings income falling into the allowance is taxed at 0%. The allowance is added to the starting rate band but reduces the basic rate and higher rate band.

- A dividend allowance of £5,000 is available to all taxpayers. Dividends falling into this band are taxed at 0%. The allowance reduces the basic rate and higher rate bands.

- Gift Aid donations and personal pension contributions are paid net of basic rate (20%) tax.

- Extend the basic rate band by the gross amount of any Gift Aid donations and/or personal pension contributions paid by the taxpayer. This gives further tax relief to higher and additional rate taxpayers.

- Payments made to charity via payroll deduction or pension contributions made to an occupational scheme are simply deducted from salary.

- Tax deducted under the PAYE system is deducted in computing tax payable and can be repaid if it is greater than the taxpayer's liability.

Keywords

- **Additional rate band:** income in excess of £150,000 is taxed here

- **Basic rate band:** the first £32,000 of income. The basic rate band may be extended by the gross amount of any Gift Aid donations and personal pension contributions paid by the taxpayer

- **Dividend allowance:** an amount of savings income that is taxed at 0%. This is £5,000 for all taxpayers

- **Higher rate band:** the next £118,000 of income. The upper limit to the higher rate band may be extended by the gross amount of any Gift Aid donations and personal pension contributions paid

- **Personal savings allowance:** an amount of savings income that is taxed at 0%. The amount varies depending on levels of income

- **Savings income starting rate band:** applies if the taxpayer has non-savings income of less than this amount and also has savings income

Activity 1: Income tax liability

	Non-savings income £	Savings income £	Total £
Employment income	35,500		35,500
Building society interest		9,000	9,000
Net income	35,500	9,000	44,500
Personal allowance	(11,000)		
Taxable income	24,500	9,000	33,500

Net income > 43,000 < £150,001 therefore £500 personal savings allowance available

		£
Non-savings income		
24,500 × 20%		4,900
Savings income		
500 × 0% (personal savings allowance)		0
7,000 × 20%		1,400
32,000		
1,500 (9,000 – 500 – 7,000) × 40%		600
Tax liability		6,900

Activity 2: Starting rate band

	Non-savings income £	Savings income £	Total £
Employment income	12,000		12,000
Bank interest		40,000	40,000
Net income	12,000	40,000	52,000
Less personal allowance	(11,000)		(11,000)
Taxable income	1,000	40,000	41,000
Net income > 42,000 < 150,000 so personal savings allowance of £500 available			
Non-savings income			
1,000 x 20%			200
Savings income:			
4,000 x 0%			0
5,000			
500 x 0% (personal savings allowance)			0
26,500 x 20%			5,300
32,000			
9,000 x 40% (40,000 – 4,000 – 500 – 26,500)			3,600
Tax liability			9,100

Activity 3: Income tax payable

	Non-savings income £	Savings income £	Dividend income £	Total £
Employment income	125,000			125,000
Bank interest		10,000		10,000
Dividends			10,000	10,000
Net income	125,000	10,000	10,000	145,000
Personal allowance	(Nil)			(Nil)
Taxable income	125,000	10,000	10,000	145,000

Note. Total income is in excess of £122,000, so Arthur is not entitled to a personal allowance. Net income is greater than £43,000 but less than £150,000 so £500 savings allowance is available. Dividend allowance is always available.

	£
Non-savings income:	
32,000 × 20%	6,400
93,000 × 40%	37,200
125,000	
Savings income:	
500 × 0% (savings allowance)	0
9,500 × 40%	3,800
10,000	
Dividend income:	
5,000 × 0%	0
5,000 × 32.5%	1,625
10,000	
Tax liability	49,025
Less PAYE	(42,000)
Tax payable	7,025

Activity 4: Tax liability with Gift Aid donation

(a) **Taxable income**

£ | 89,000 |

Workings

Taxable income

	Non savings income £
Employment income	100,000
Less personal allowance (income ≤ 100,000 ∴ no restriction)	(11,000)
Taxable income	89,000

(b) **Tax liability if he does not make the donation**

£ | 29,200 |

Workings

Tax liability without the donation

	£
32,000 × 20%	6,400
57,000 × 40%	22,800
89,000	
Tax liability	29,200

(c) **Tax liability if he does make the donation**

£ | 27,200 |

Workings

Tax liability with the donation

	£
Gross donation is $8,000 \times \dfrac{100}{80} =$	10,000
Basic rate extends to 10,000 + 32,000 =	42,000
42,000 × 20%	8,400
47,000 × 40%	18,800
89,000	
	27,200

(d) Tax saved if he does make the donation

£ | 4,000 |

Workings

Tax saving (29,200 – 27,200)	= extra 2,000
which is 20% of the gross donation	
(8,000 × 100/80 = 10,000 @ 20%)	
Total relief:	
Obtained at source: 10,000 – 8,000 =	2,000
Reduction in tax liability (above)	2,000
Total	4,000
ie 40% of gross donation of 10,000	

Test your learning

1   **At what rates is income tax charged on non-savings income? Tick ONE box.**

	✓
0%, 20%, 40% and 45%	
40% and 45%	
20% only	
20%, 40% and 45%	

2   In 2016/17 Albert has a salary of £16,600, £2,000 of building society interest and £3,000 of dividends.

   Albert's income tax liability is:

   £ _____

3   In 2016/17 Carol has a salary of £5,000, and has received building society interest of £18,000 and a dividend of £22,000.

   Carol's income tax liability is:

   £ _____

4   In 2016/17 Harry has a salary of £140,000, and has received building society interest of £20,000 and dividends of £30,000.

   Harry's income tax liability is:

   £ _____

5   **Explain how tax relief is given on Gift Aid donations.**

6   Doreen has the following sources of income in 2016/17.

	£
Gross pension income (tax deducted under PAYE £2,010)	17,000
Property income	3,500
Interest received from government stock	380
Dividends received	700
Premium bond prize	100

   Calculate Doreen's income tax payable for the year.

7   Sase has the following income and outgoings in 2016/17.

	£
Business profits	36,600
Building society interest received	2,000
Dividends received	8,000
Gift Aid donation paid	1,600

Compute Sase's income tax payable for the year.

8   Vince is a higher rate taxpayer and makes a Gift Aid donation of £15,000 in 2016/17.

What is Vince's basic rate band in 2016/17?

Tick ONE box.

	✓
£32,000	
£47,000	
£50,750	
£57,000	

Chargeable gains

7

Learning outcomes

4.1K	Identify the main features of the capital gains tax system
4.2K	Describe chargeable and exempt assets
4.3K	Describe the process for relief of current year allowable losses and for losses unrelieved in the current year
4.4K	Identify the current annual exempt amount and describe the effect of this on an individual's capital gains tax liability
4.5S	Identify and value chargeable personal assets that have been disposed of
4.6S	Calculate chargeable gains and allowable losses
4.7S	Apply reliefs and exemptions
4.8S	Calculate capital gains tax payable
5.2S	Record relevant details of gains and the capital gains tax payable in the tax return

Assessment context

The material in this chapter will be tested in Task 9 of the CBT for 12 marks and Task 11 for 6 marks. Make sure that you can perform all the calculations shown in this chapter. Task 8 requires you to complete a tax return for 7 marks and this could be the capital gains tax page.

Qualification context

You will not see the information in this chapter outside of this unit unless you are also studying *Business Tax*.

Business context

People sell assets for a variety of reasons. It is important to realise when a charge to capital gains tax arises and when capital gains tax needs to be paid if a taxpayer is to avoid paying interest and penalties.

Chapter overview

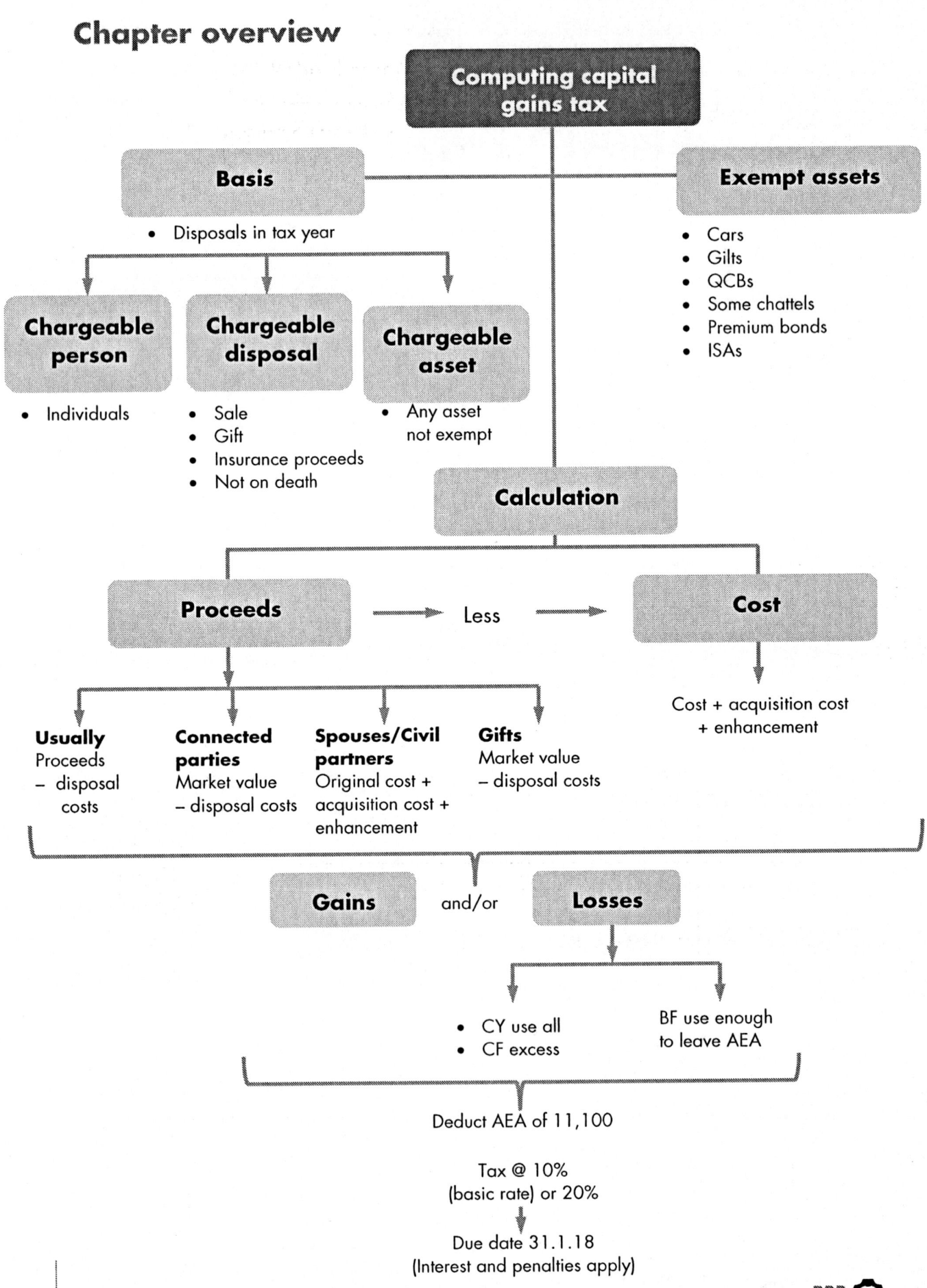

Computing capital gains tax

Basis

- Disposals in tax year

Chargeable person

- Individuals

Chargeable disposal

- Sale
- Gift
- Insurance proceeds
- Not on death

Chargeable asset

- Any asset not exempt

Exempt assets

- Cars
- Gilts
- QCBs
- Some chattels
- Premium bonds
- ISAs

Calculation

Proceeds → Less → **Cost**

Usually
Proceeds
– disposal costs

Connected parties
Market value
– disposal costs

Spouses/Civil partners
Original cost +
acquisition cost +
enhancement

Gifts
Market value
– disposal costs

Cost + acquisition cost
+ enhancement

Gains and/or **Losses**

- CY use all
- CF excess

BF use enough
to leave AEA

Deduct AEA of 11,100

Tax @ 10%
(basic rate) or 20%

Due date 31.1.18
(Interest and penalties apply)

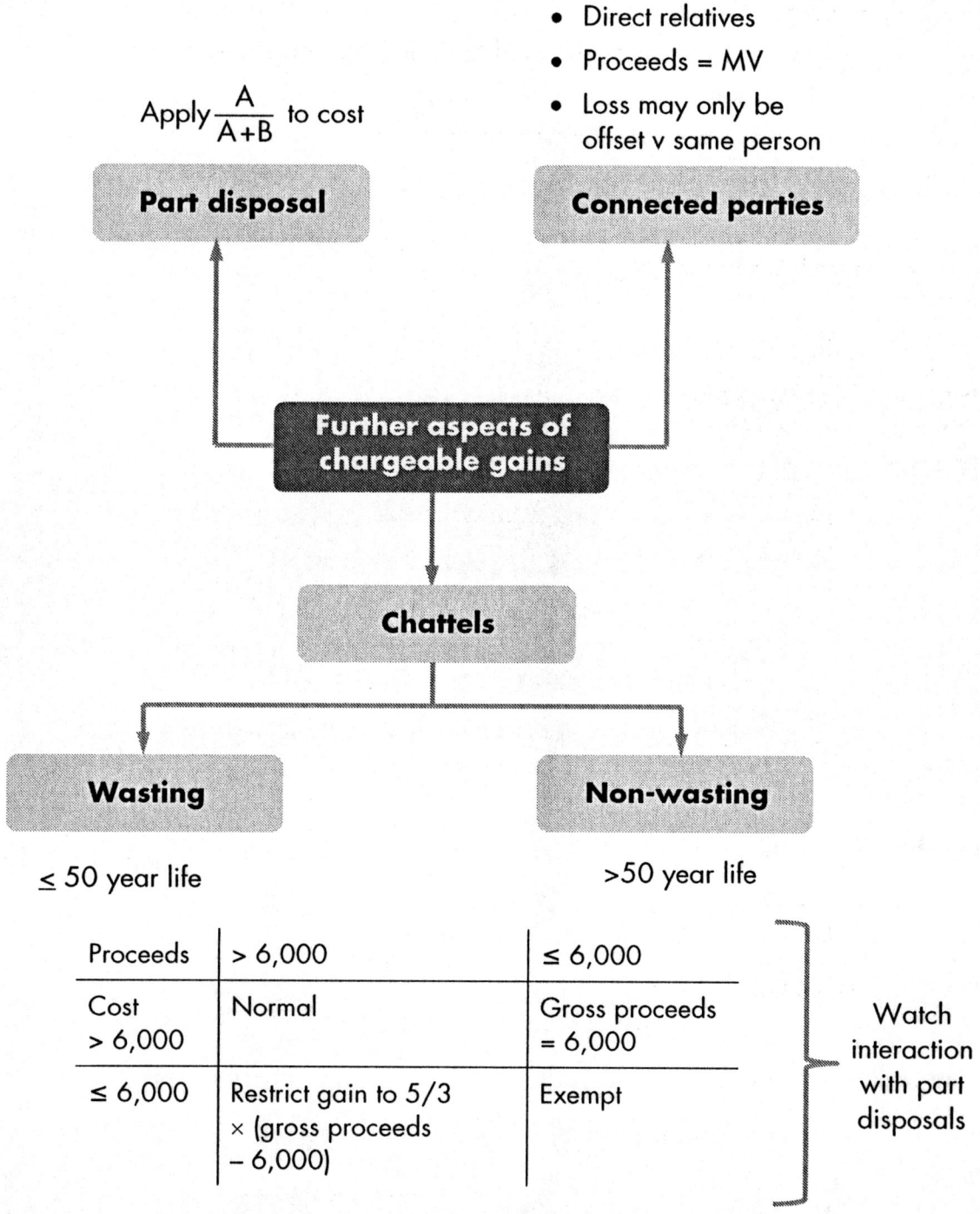

Apply $\dfrac{A}{A+B}$ to cost

Part disposal

- Direct relatives
- Proceeds = MV
- Loss may only be offset v same person

Connected parties

Further aspects of chargeable gains

Chattels

Wasting

$\leq$ 50 year life

Non-wasting

>50 year life

Proceeds	> 6,000	$\leq$ 6,000
Cost > 6,000	Normal	Gross proceeds = 6,000
$\leq$ 6,000	Restrict gain to 5/3 × (gross proceeds – 6,000)	Exempt

Watch interaction with part disposals

Introduction

Income is a regular receipt that is expected to recur. A gain is a one-off disposal of a capital item.

Individuals pay **income tax** on income and **capital gains tax** on capital gains.

1 When does a chargeable gain arise?

For a disposable to be taxable there must be a **chargeable disposal** of a **chargeable asset** by a **chargeable person**.

1.1 Chargeable person

Individuals are chargeable persons.

1.2 Chargeable disposal

An individual is taxed on gains arising from disposals in the current tax year.

The following are the most important **chargeable disposals**:

- Sales of assets or parts of assets
- Gifts of assets or parts of assets
- The loss or destruction of an asset

A chargeable disposal occurs on the date of the contract (where there is one, whether written or oral), or the date of a conditional contract becoming unconditional.

Exempt disposals include:

- Transfers on death
- Gifts to charities

On death the heirs inherit assets as if they bought them at death for their then market values. There is no capital gain or allowable loss on death.

1.3 Chargeable assets

All assets are chargeable unless they are classified as exempt. The following are exempt:

- Motor vehicles suitable for private use
- UK government stocks (gilt-edged securities)
- Qualifying corporate bonds (company loan stock)
- **Wasting chattels** (greyhounds, racehorses) (see later)
- Premium bonds
- Investments held in an ISA

Assessment focus point

Make sure you identify an exempt asset, state that it is exempt in the exam and do not tax it.

2 Calculation of chargeable gains and allowable losses

Illustration 1: Basic capital gains computation

Disposal consideration (or market value)	X
Less incidental costs of disposal	(X)
Net proceeds	**X**
Less allowable cost (including acquisition cost)	(X)
Less enhancement expenditure	(X)
Capital gain / (capital loss)	**X/(X)**

We now look at each of the items in the above proforma in turn.

2.1 Disposal consideration

Usually this is proceeds received. Note, though, that a disposal is deemed to take place at market value when the disposal is:

- A gift
- Made for a consideration that cannot be valued
- Deliberately sold for a consideration of less than market value
- Made to a connected person (see later)

Note that if a taxpayer makes a sale to an unconnected person and strikes a bad bargain then the actual proceeds achieved will be used. Market value is only used for a sale between unconnected persons when the taxpayer deliberately chooses to sell at undervalue to give the buyer a benefit.

2.2 Costs

The following costs are deducted in the above proforma:

(a) **Incidental costs of disposal**

These are the costs of selling an asset. They may include advertising costs, estate agents' fees, legal costs and valuation fees. These costs should be deducted separately from any other allowable costs.

(b) **Allowable costs**

These include:

(i) The original purchase price of the asset
(ii) Costs incurred in purchasing the asset (estate agents' fees, legal fees, etc)

(c) Enhancement expenditure

This is capital expenditure which enhances the value of the asset and is reflected in the state or nature of the asset at the time of disposal.

Illustration 2: Calculation of capital gain

Jack bought a holiday cottage for £25,000. He paid legal costs of £600 on the purchase.

Jack spent £8,000 building an extension to the cottage.

Jack sold the cottage for £60,000. He paid estate agents' fees of £1,200 and legal costs of £750.

Jack's gain on sale is:

£	24,450

	£
Disposal consideration	60,000
Less incidental costs of disposal (1,200 + 750)	(1,950)
Net proceeds	58,050
Less allowable costs (25,000 + 600)	(25,600)
Less enhancement expenditure	(8,000)
Chargeable gain	24,450

Activity 1: Capital gain calculation

Mr Dunstable bought an asset for £15,000 in February 1986. He incurred legal fees of £500. He sold the asset for £38,500 incurring expenses of £1,500. While he owned the asset he improved it at a cost of £3,000.

Required

Complete the table showing Mr Dunstable's gain.

Solution

	£
Proceeds	
Less selling expenses	
Net proceeds	
Less cost	
Less legal fees on purchase	
Less enhancement	
Capital gain	

3 Computing taxable gains in a tax year

An individual pays capital gains tax (CGT) on any **taxable gains** arising in a **tax year** (6 April to 5 April).

All the chargeable gains made in the tax year are added together, and any capital losses made in the same tax year are deducted to give net gains (or losses) for the year. Next we deduct any unrelieved capital losses brought forward from previous years. Finally the annual exempt amount is deducted to arrive at taxable gains, on which CGT will be applied.

Illustration 3: Year-end computation

	£
Current gains	X
Current losses (all)	(X)
Net gains	X
Losses b/fwd from earlier years (restricted)	(X)
Net capital gains	X
Annual exempt amount	(11,100)
Taxable gains	X

Unused annual exempt amounts cannot be carried forward.

3.1 Annual exempt amount

Key term

Annual exempt amount	This is the amount of capital gains a taxpayer may realise in a tax year before they have to pay capital gains tax.
	For 2016/17 it is £11,100.
	It is also known as the annual exemption.

All individuals are entitled to an annual exempt amount. As you can see above, it is the last deduction to be made in computing taxable gains, and effectively means that for 2016/17 the first £11,100 of chargeable gains is tax free for an individual.

3.2 Losses

If losses have been made in the current year they must be offset against the gains of that year even if this means that some or all of the annual exempt amount is wasted.

If the losses in a year are greater than the gains then the excess losses are carried forward.

When a capital loss is carried forward it is set against net gains in the next tax year but only to reduce the net gains in the next tax year down to the level of the annual exempt amount. This means the taxpayer does not lose the benefit of the annual exempt amount.

Any further loss remaining is carried forward.

Illustration 4: Capital losses

(a) Tim has chargeable gains for 2016/17 of £25,000 and allowable losses of £16,000. As the losses are current year losses they must be fully relieved against the gains to produce net gains of £9,000, despite the fact that net gains are below the annual exempt amount.

	£
Chargeable gains in tax year	25,000
Less losses in tax year	(16,000)
Net chargeable gains	9,000
Less annual exempt amount	(11,100)
Taxable gain	0

(b) Hattie has gains of £11,600 for 2016/17 and allowable losses brought forward of £6,000. Hattie restricts her loss relief to £500 so as to leave net gains of (£11,600 – £500) = £11,100, which will be exactly covered by the annual exempt amount for 2016/17.

	£
Net chargeable gains	11,600
Less losses brought forward	(500)
Less annual exempt amount	(11,100)
Taxable gain	0

The remaining £5,500 of losses will be carried forward to 2017/18.

Activity 2: Current year losses

In 2016/17, Ted makes gains of £45,000 and £10,000. He also makes a loss of £48,000. Ted has no losses to bring forward from earlier years.

Required

Complete the following sentences:

Ted's net capital gain for 2016/17 before the annual exempt amount is

£ [　　　　　　　　]

Ted has a loss to carry forward of £ [　　　　　　　　]

Activity 3: Prior year losses

Tara makes a gain on a property in 2016/17 of £12,000 (proceeds of £25,000 less cost of £13,000). She makes no other disposals in the tax year. Tara has losses brought forward from the previous year of £10,000.

Required

Complete the following sentences:

Tara's net capital gain for 2016/17 before the annual exempt amount is

£ [　　　　　　　　]

Tara has a loss to carry forward of £ [　　　　　　　　]

4 Computing capital gains tax (CGT) payable

An individual's taxable gains are chargeable to CGT at the rate of 10% or 20% depending on the individual's taxable income for 2016/17.

If the individual is a basic rate taxpayer, then CGT is payable at 10% on an amount of taxable gains up to the amount of the taxpayer's **unused** basic rate band and at 20% on the excess.

If the individual is a higher or additional rate taxpayer, then CGT is payable at 20% on all their taxable gains. Note the basic rate band covers taxable income and gains up to £32,000 (for 2016/17).

Note that a large gain may take a taxpayer out of the basic rate band and into the higher rate band. Don't forget that the bands will be extended by Gift Aid and/or personal pension scheme contributions.

Illustration 5: Calculating capital gains tax

(a) Sally has taxable income (ie the amount after the deduction of the personal allowance) of £10,000 in 2016/17 and made taxable gains (ie gains after deduction of the annual exempt amount) of £20,000 in 2016/17.

Sally's CGT liability is:

£20,000 × 10%   £2,000

The taxable income uses £10,000 of the basic rate band, leaving £22,000 of the basic rate band unused, therefore all of the taxable gain is taxed at 10%.

(b) Hector has taxable income of £50,000 in 2016/17 (ie he is a higher rate taxpayer). He made taxable gains of £10,000 in 2016/17.

Hector's CGT liability is:

£10,000 × 20%   £2,000

All of Hector's basic rate band has been taken up by the taxable income, therefore the taxable gain is taxed at 20%.

(c) Isabel has taxable income of £30,000 in 2016/17 and made taxable gains of £25,000 in 2016/17.

Isabel has (£32,000 – £30,000) = £2,000 of her basic rate band unused. Isabel's CGT liability is:

	£
2,000 × 10%	200
23,000 × 20%	4,600
25,000	4,800

Activity 4: Computing capital gains tax payable

Mr Dunstable (see Activity 1) had a chargeable gain of £18,500 in 2016/17. He has taxable income of £31,000.

Required

What is Mr Dunstable's capital gains tax payable?

£ [   ]

5 Self-assessment for CGT

5.1 Administration

CGT is payable on 31 January following the end of the tax year.

There are no payments on account.

An individual taxpayer who makes chargeable gains in a tax year is usually required to file details of the gains in a tax return. In many cases, the taxpayer will be filing a tax return for income tax purposes and will include the capital gains supplementary pages. If, however, the taxpayer only has chargeable gains to report, **they must notify their chargeability to HMRC by 5 October following the end of the tax year**.

The consequences of late notification, late filing, late payment of CGT and errors are the same as for income tax so penalties and interest may be charged where applicable. Repayment interest may be paid on overpayments of CGT.

5.2 CGT return page

In the exam you may have to complete the CGT summary page from the tax return.

This is included below showing the figures from the earlier activity featuring Tara (Activity 3: Prior year losses) for illustration purposes.

HM Revenue & Customs

Capital gains summary
Tax year 6 April 2016 to 5 April 2017 (2016-17)

1 Your name

Tara

2 Your Unique Taxpayer Reference (UTR)

Summary of your enclosed computations

Please read the 'Capital gains summary notes' before filling in this section. **You must enclose your computations, including details of each gain or loss, as well as filling in the boxes.**

ⓘ To get notes and helpsheets that will help you fill in this form, go to www.gov.uk/self-assessment-forms-and-helpsheets

3 Total gains (boxes 21 + 27 + 33 + 34)

£ 12000 · 00

4 Gains qualifying for Entrepreneurs' Relief (but excluding gains deferred from before 23 June 2010) - read the notes

£ · 00

5 Gains invested under Seed Enterprise Investment Scheme and qualifying for relief - read the notes

£ · 00

6 Total losses of the year - enter '0' if there are none

£ · 00

7 Losses brought forward and used in the year

£ 900 · 00

8 Adjustment to Capital Gains Tax - read the notes

£ · 00

9 Additional liability for non-resident or dual resident trusts

£ · 00

10 Losses available to be carried forward to later years

£ 9100 · 00

11 Losses used against an earlier year's gain (special circumstances apply - read the notes)

£ · 00

12 Share loss relief used against income - amount claimed against 2016-17 income - read the notes

£ · 00

13 Amount in box 12 relating to share loss relief to which Enterprise Investment Scheme/Seed Enterprise Investment Scheme relief is attributable

£ · 00

14 Losses used against income - amount claimed against 2015-16 income - read the notes

£ · 00

15 Amount in box 14 relating to shares to which Enterprise Investment Scheme/Seed Enterprise Investment Scheme relief is attributable

£ · 00

16 Income losses of 2016-17 set against gains

£ · 00

17 Deferred gains from before 23 June 2010 qualifying for Entrepreneurs' Relief

£ · 00

(Adapted from HMRC, 2016)

6 Special rules applying to specific disposals

Assessment focus point

The following rules need to be used in particular circumstances. Make sure you spot them in the assessment and apply them when required.

6.1 Part disposals and chattels

6.1.1 Part disposals

Sometimes part, rather than the whole, of an asset is disposed of. For instance, one-third of a piece of land may be sold. In this case, we need to be able to compute the chargeable gain or allowable loss arising on the part of the asset disposed of.

The problem is that, although we know what the disposal proceeds are for the part of the asset disposed of, we do not usually know what proportion of the 'cost' of the whole asset relates to that part. The solution to this is to **use the following fraction to determine the cost of the part disposed of**.

Formula to learn

The fraction is:

$$\frac{A}{A+B} = \frac{\text{Value of the part disposed of}}{\text{Value of the part disposed of} + \text{Market value of the remainder}}$$

A   is the 'gross' proceeds (or market value) before deducting incidental costs of disposal.

B   is the market value of the part of the asset that was not sold.

Illustration 6: Part disposal calculation

	£
Gross proceeds	X
Less selling costs	(X)
	X
Less:	
Original cost of the whole asset $\times \dfrac{A}{A+B}$	(C)
Gain	**X**

Illustration 7: Part disposal

Mr Jones bought 4 acres of land for £270,000. He sold 1 acre of the land at auction for £200,000, before auction expenses of 15%. The market value of the 3 remaining acres is £460,000.

The cost of the land being sold is:

$$\frac{200,000}{200,000+460,000} \times £270,000 = £81,818$$

	£
Disposal proceeds	200,000
Less incidental costs of sale (15% × £200,000)	(30,000)
Net proceeds	170,000
Less cost (see above)	(81,818)
Chargeable gain	88,182

Activity 5: Part disposal

Tom bought 10 acres of land for £20,000.

He sold 3 acres of land for £10,000 incurring disposal costs of £950 when the remaining 7 acres were worth £36,000.

Required

Complete the following sentences:

The gain on the disposal of the land is £ [   ]

The cost of the remaining land carried forward is £ [   ]

6.1.2 Chattels

Key term

Chattels	are tangible moveable property.
Wasting chattel	is a chattel with an estimated remaining useful life of 50 years or less, eg a racehorse or greyhound.

Wasting chattels are exempt from CGT so there are no chargeable gains and no allowable losses.

Non-wasting chattels are chargeable to CGT in the normal way, subject to the following exceptions/restrictions.

Illustration 8: Rule for computing gains/losses on non-wasting chattels

≤ 6,000	≤ 6,000	Wholly exempt	• No need to calculate any gain
≤ 6,000	> 6,000	Any gain restricted to max of: $\frac{5}{3}$ (Gross proceeds – £6,000)	• Calculate gain, compare to the maximum, take the lower figure
> 6,000	≤ 6,000	Gross proceeds deemed to be £6,000	• Do normal calculation but always use £6,000 as gross proceeds figure
> 6,000	> 6,000	Wholly taxable	• Calculate a gain using the normal rules

Illustration 9: Proceeds > £6,000 cost < £6,000

John purchased a painting for £3,000. On 1 January 2017 he sold the painting at auction.

If the gross sale proceeds are £4,000, the gain on sale will be exempt.

If the gross sale proceeds are £8,000 with costs of sale of 10%, the gain arising on the disposal of the painting will be calculated as follows:

	£
Gross proceeds	8,000
Less incidental costs of sale (10% × £8,000)	(800)
Net proceeds	7,200
Less cost	(3,000)
Chargeable gain	4,200
Gain cannot exceed 5/3 × £(8,000 – 6,000)	3,333

Therefore chargeable gain is £3,333.

Illustration 10: Proceeds < £6,000 cost > £6,000

Magee purchased an antique desk for £8,000. She sold the desk in an auction for £4,750 net of auctioneer's fees of 5% in November 2016.

Magee obviously has a loss and therefore the allowable loss is calculated on deemed proceeds of £6,000. The costs of disposal can be deducted from the deemed proceeds of £6,000.

	£
Deemed disposal proceeds	6,000
Less incidental costs of disposal (£4,750 × 5/95)	(250)
	5,750
Less cost	(8,000)
Allowable loss	(2,250)

Activity 6: Chattels

(a)   Orlando Gibbons purchased a rare manuscript for £500. He sold it several years later for £9,000, before deducting the auctioneer's commission of £1,000.

(b)   He also had an antique bought for £7,000 which he sold 2 years later for £3,000.

Required

Complete the following sentences:

(a)   The chargeable gain on the disposal is £ [   ]

(b)   The loss on the disposal is £ [   ]

6.1.3 Interaction of chattels and part disposals

When the part disposal rules are applied to the sale of 'part of an asset', the allocation of the cost between the part disposed of and the remaining asset may then result in the need to consider the chattels rules. The rules only apply to chattels and not, for example, the part disposal of land (which is not tangible moveable property).

Assessment focus point

This is a minor point which is less likely to be tested in your assessment.

Illustration 11: Part disposal of chattels

Terry bought a set of 24 Dickens characters for £18,000. He sold 6 for £8,000 when the remaining 18 were valued at £26,500.

	£
Proceeds	8,000
Cost	
$18,000 \times \dfrac{8,000}{8,000+26,500}$	(4,174)
	3,826
Non-wasting chattel proceeds > 6,000, cost ≤ 6,000	
Restricted to	
$\dfrac{5}{3} \times (8,000 - 6,000) =$	3,333
Tax	3,333
Cost c/f 18,000 – 4,174	13,826

6.2 Transfers to connected persons

If a disposal by an individual is made to a connected person, **the disposal is deemed to take place at the market value of the asset.**

If an **allowable loss arises** on the disposal, it can **only be set against gains** arising in the same or future tax years from disposals **to the same connected person**, and the loss can only be set off if they are still connected with the person making the loss.

For this purpose an individual is connected with:

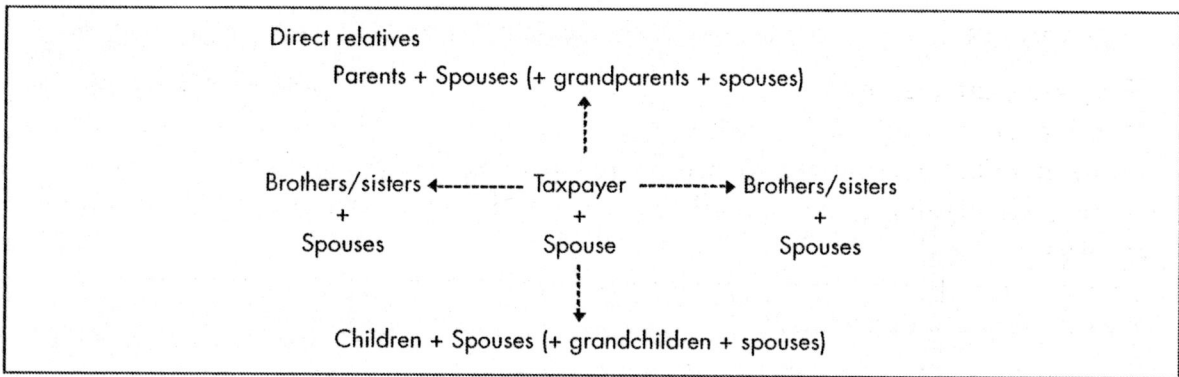

6.3 Transfers between spouses/civil partners

Spouses/civil partners are taxed as two separate people. Each individual has an annual exempt amount, and allowable losses of one individual cannot be set against gains of the other.

Disposals between spouses/civil partners do not give rise to chargeable gains or allowable losses. The disposal is said to be on a **'no gain/no loss'** basis. The acquiring spouse/civil partner takes the base cost of the disposing spouse/civil partner.

Activity 7: Transfers between spouses/civil partners

William sold an asset to his wife Kate in May 2015 for £32,000 when its market value was £45,000. William acquired the asset for £14,000 in June 2005.

Required

Calculate the chargeable gain on this transfer. Tick ONE box.

	✓
Nil	
£18,000	
£31,000	
£13,000	

Chapter summary

- A chargeable gain arises when there is a chargeable disposal of a chargeable asset by a chargeable person.

- Enhancement expenditure can be deducted in computing a chargeable gain if it is reflected in the state and nature of the asset at the time of disposal.

- Taxable gains are net chargeable gains for a tax year (ie minus allowable losses of the current tax year and any unrelieved capital losses brought forward) minus the annual exempt amount.

- Losses brought forward can only reduce net chargeable gains down to the amount of the annual exempt amount.

- The rates of CGT are 10% and 20%, but the lower rate of 10% only applies if and to the extent that the individual has any unused basic rate band.

- CGT is payable by 31 January following the end of the tax year.

- There is a special page to complete for capital gains on the tax return.

- CGT is self-assessed and has the same rules about notification of chargeability, penalties and interest as income tax.

- On the part disposal of an asset the formula $A/(A + B)$ must be applied to work out the cost attributable to the part disposed of.

- Wasting chattels are exempt assets (eg racehorses and greyhounds).

- If a non-wasting chattel is sold for gross proceeds of £6,000 or less and was bought for £6,000 or less then any gain arising is exempt.

- If gross proceeds exceed £6,000 on the sale of a non-wasting chattel but the cost is less than £6,000, any gain arising on the disposal of the asset is limited to $5/3 \times$ (Gross proceeds − £6,000).

- If the gross proceeds are less than £6,000 on the sale of a non-wasting chattel but it was bought for more than £6,000 any loss otherwise arising is restricted by deeming the gross proceeds to be £6,000.

- A disposal to a connected person takes place at market value.

- For individuals, connected people are broadly brothers, sisters, lineal ancestors and descendants and their spouses/civil partners plus similar relations of a spouse/civil partner.

- Losses on disposals to connected people can only be set against gains on disposals to the same connected person.

- Disposals between spouses/civil partners take place on a no gain/no loss basis.

- **Chargeable asset:** any asset that is not an exempt asset
- **Chargeable disposal:** a sale or gift of an asset
- **Chargeable person:** an individual or company
- **Chattel:** tangible moveable property
- **Connected person:** a close relation of the taxpayer or their spouse/civil partner
- **Enhancement expenditure:** capital expenditure that enhances the value of the asset and is reflected in the state or nature of the asset at the time of disposal
- **Exempt disposal:** a disposal on which no chargeable gain or allowable loss arises
- **Part disposal:** when part of an, rather than a whole, asset is disposed of
- **Taxable gains:** the chargeable gains of an individual for a tax year, after deducting allowable losses of the same tax year, any unrelieved capital losses brought forward and the annual exempt amount
- **Wasting chattel:** a chattel with an estimated remaining useful life of 50 years or less

Activity answers

Activity 1: Capital gain calculation

	£
Proceeds	38,500
Less selling expenses	(1,500)
Net proceeds	37,000
Less cost	(15,000)
Less legal fees on purchase	(500)
Less enhancement	(3,000)
Capital gain	18,500

Activity 2: Current year losses

Ted's net capital gain for 2016/17 before the annual exempt amount is

£ | 7,000 |

Ted has a loss to carry forward of £ | nil |

Workings

	£
Gains 45,000 + 10,000	55,000
Less loss	(48,000)
Net capital gains	7,000
Less annual exempt amount	(11,100)
Taxable gains	Nil
The balance of the annual exempt amount is wasted.	

Activity 3: Prior year losses

Tara's net capital gain for 2016/17 before the annual exempt amount is

£ 11,100

Tara has a loss to carry forward of £ 9,100

Workings

	£
Gain of 2016/17	12,000
Less losses b/f (bal)	(900)
Net gain	11,100
Less annual exempt amount	(11,100)
Taxable gains	Nil
Losses to c/f £(10,000 – 900)	9,100

Activity 4: Computing capital gains tax payable

Mr Dunstable's capital gains tax payable is £ 1,380

Workings

	£
Capital gain	18,500
Less annual exempt amount	(11,100)
Taxable gain	7,400
Basic rate band	32,000
Taxable income	(31,000)
Basic rate band remaining	1,000

	£
Capital gains tax payable	
1,000 × 10%	100
6,400 × 20%	1,280
7,400	1,380

Activity 5: Part disposal

The gain on the disposal of the land is £ | 4,702

The cost of the remaining land carried forward is £ | 15,652

Workings

	£
Gross proceeds	10,000
Less disposal costs	(950)
Net proceeds	9,050
Cost $\dfrac{10}{10+36} \times 20,000$	(4,348)
	4,702
Cost of remaining land for future CGT calculations: = 20,000 – 4,348	15,652

Activity 6: Chattels

(a)   The chargeable gain on the disposal is £ | 5,000

Workings

Non-wasting chattel: cost ≤ £6,000, proceeds > £6,000	£
Proceeds	9,000
Less commission	(1,000)
Net proceeds	8,000
Less cost	(500)
Capital gain	7,500
$\dfrac{5}{3}$ (Gross proceeds – 6,000)	
$= \dfrac{5}{3}$ (9,000 – 6,000)	
= 5,000	
∴ take lower gain 5,000	5,000

(b) The loss on the disposal is £ | 1,000 |

Workings

Non-wasting chattel: cost > £6,000, proceeds ≤ £6,000	£
Proceeds (deemed)	6,000
Less cost	(7,000)
Allowable loss	(1,000)

Activity 7: transfers between spouses/civil partners

The chargeable gain on transfer is:

	✓
Nil	✓
£18,000	
£31,000	
£13,000	

The transfer takes place at no gain/no loss and Kate assumes the base cost of £14,000 as her cost.

Test your learning

1   **Tick to show if the following disposals would be chargeable or exempt for CGT.**

	Chargeable ✓	Exempt ✓
A gift of an antique necklace		
The sale of a building		
Sale of a racehorse		

2   Janet bought a plot of land in July 2006 for £80,000. She spent £10,000 on drainage in April 2009. She sold the land for £200,000 in August 2016.

Using the proforma layout provided, compute the gain on sale.

	£
Proceeds of sale	
Less cost	
Less enhancement expenditure	
Chargeable gain	

3   Philip has chargeable gains of £171,000 and allowable losses of £5,300 in 2016/17. Losses brought forward at 6 April 2016 amount to £10,000.

The amount liable to CGT in 2016/17 is:

£

The losses carried forward are:

£

4   Martha is a higher rate taxpayer who made chargeable gains (before the annual exempt amount) of £23,900 in October 2016.

Martha's CGT liability for 2016/17 is:

£

5   **The payment date for capital gains tax for 2016/17 is (insert date XX/XX/XXXX):**

6   **Tick to show the correct answer.**

Richard sells 4 acres of land (out of a plot of 10 acres) for £38,000 in July 2016. Costs of disposal amount to £3,000. The 10-acre plot cost £41,500. The market value of the 6 acres remaining is £48,000.

The chargeable gain/allowable loss arising is:

	✓
£16,663	
£17,500	
£19,663	
£18,337	

7   Mustafa bought a non-wasting chattel for £3,500.

   The gain arising if he sells it for:

   (a) £5,800 after deducting selling expenses of £180 is:

   £ [   ]

   (b) £8,200 after deducting selling expenses of £220 is:

   £ [   ]

8   **Decide whether the following statement is true or false.**

A loss arising on a disposal to a connected person can be set against any gains arising in the same tax year or in subsequent tax years.

	✓
True	
False	

9   **Decide whether the following statement is true or false.**

No gain or loss arises on a disposal to a spouse/civil partner.

	✓
True	
False	

10 **Complete the table by ticking the appropriate box for each scenario.**

	Actual proceeds used	Deemed proceeds (market value) used	No gain or loss basis
Paul sells an asset to his civil partner Joe for £3,600.			
Grandmother gives an asset to her grandchild worth £1,000.			
Sarah sells an asset worth £20,000 to her best friend Cathy for £12,000. Sarah knows the asset is worth £20,000.			

Share disposals

8

Learning outcomes

4.5S	Identify and value chargeable assets and shares that have been disposed of

Assessment context

Shares will be tested for 8 marks in Task 10 of the CBT. The task will be assessed by free data entry of all workings and will be human marked.

Qualification context

Share disposals by individuals also feature in *Business Tax*. You will not see these rules anywhere else in your qualification.

Business context

A tax practitioner needs to be able to calculate capital gains tax payable on the disposal of shares for their clients.

Chapter overview

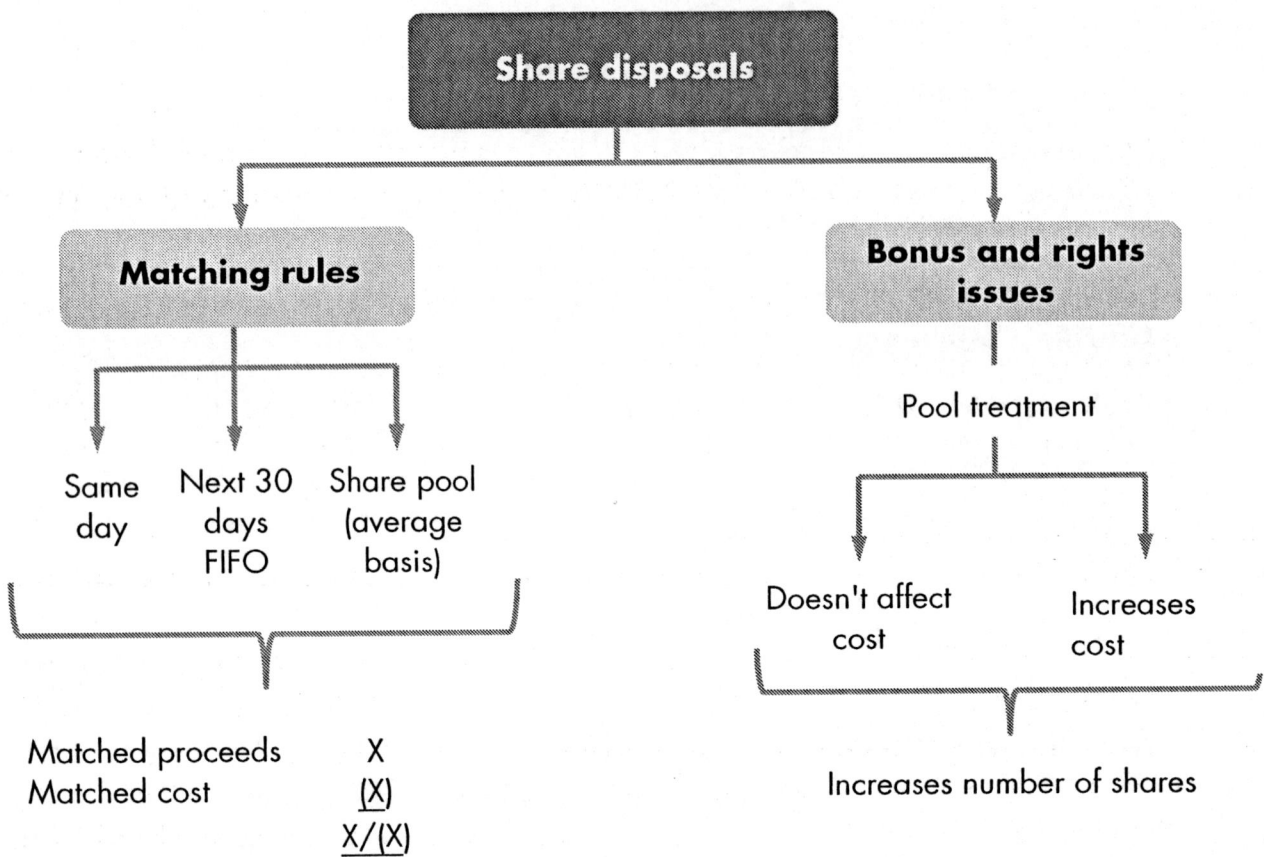

Share disposals

Matching rules

- Same day
- Next 30 days FIFO
- Share pool (average basis)

Matched proceeds	X
Matched cost	(X)
	X/(X)

Bonus and rights issues

Pool treatment

- Doesn't affect cost
- Increases cost

Increases number of shares

Introduction

In this chapter we're going to look at special rules that apply when shares are sold.

1 Share disposal rules

1.1 Matching rules

Shares present special problems when computing gains or losses on disposal. For instance, suppose that a taxpayer buys some shares in X plc on the following dates:

	No of shares	Cost £
5 July 1992	150	195
17 January 1997	100	375
2 July 2016	100	1,000

On 15 June 2016, he sells 220 of his shares for £3,300. **To work out his chargeable gain, we need to be able to identify which shares** out of his three holdings **were actually sold**. Since one share is identical to any other, it is not possible to work this out by reference to factual evidence.

As a result, it has been necessary to devise 'matching rules'. These allow us to identify on a disposal which shares have been sold and so **work out what the allowable cost** (and therefore the gain) **on disposal should be**. These matching rules are considered in detail below.

Assessment focus point

It is very important that you understand the matching rules. These rules are very regularly assessed and if you do not understand them you will not be able to get any part of the task right.

Matching rules

Shares sold should be matched with purchases in the following order:

(1) Acquisitions on the same day as disposal.

(2) Acquisitions within the following 30 days on a first in, first out (FIFO) basis.

(3) Shares from the share pool. The share pool includes all other shares not acquired on the dates above, and is explained below.

Illustration 1: Matching rules

Noah acquired shares in Ark Ltd as follows.

2 August 2012   10,000 shares
25 April 2014   10,000 shares
17 June 2016   1,000 shares
19 June 2016   2,000 shares

Noah sold 15,000 shares on 17 June 2016.

Which shares is he selling for capital gains tax purposes?

Noah will match his disposal of 15,000 shares on 17 June 2016 as follows:

(1)   1,000 shares bought on 17 June 2016 (same day)
(2)   2,000 shares bought on 19 June 2016 (next 30 days, FIFO basis)
(3)   12,000 shares from the 20,000 shares in the share pool

Illustration 2: Basic computation

	£	£
For each batch of matched shares:		
Proportion of proceeds	X	
Less cost (if from share pool W1)	(X)	
		X

(W1)   Share pool

	No of shares	Cost £
Shares bought/sold	X	X

1.2 Share pool

The share pool includes shares acquired up to the day before the disposal on which we are calculating the gain or loss. It grows when an acquisition is made and shrinks when a disposal is made.

The calculation of the share pool value

To compute the value of the share pool, set up two columns of figures:

(1)   The number of shares
(2)   The cost of the shares

Each time shares are acquired, both the number and the cost of the acquired shares are added to those already in the pool.

When there is a disposal from the pool, both the number of shares being disposed of and a cost relating to those shares are deducted from the pool. The cost of the disposal is calculated as a proportion of total cost in the pool, based on the number of shares being sold.

Illustration 3: The share pool

Jackie bought 10,000 shares in X plc for £6,000 in August 1996 and another 10,000 shares for £9,000 in December 2008.

She sold 12,000 shares for £24,000 in August 2016.

The gain is:

	£
Proceeds of sale	24,000
Less allowable cost (W1)	(9,000)
Chargeable gain	15,000

(W1) The share pool is:

	No of shares	Cost £
August 1996 acquisition	10,000	6,000
December 2008 acquisition	10,000	9,000
	20,000	15,000
August 2016 disposal (£15,000 × 12,000/20,000 = £9,000)	(12,000)	(9,000)
c/f	8,000	6,000

Activity 1: Matching rules

Mr L made the following purchases of ordinary shares in H plc:

Date	Number	Cost
15 May 2002	2,200	8,800
1 May 2016	400	3,000
17 May 2016	500	4,500

On 1 May 2016 Mr L sold 1,600 shares for £14,000.

Required

What is the chargeable gain or loss for 2016/17 on the disposal of these shares? Clearly show the balance of shares to be carried forward.

Solution

	Number	£

Activity 2: Share pool

Mr Lambert purchased the following holdings in Grande plc:

Date	Number	Cost £
January 1985	3,000	5,000
February 1987	1,000	4,000

In May 2016 he sold 2,000 shares for £14,000.

Required

What is the chargeable gain or loss for 2016/17 on the disposal of these shares? Clearly show the balance of shares to be carried forward.

Solution

	Number	£

1.3 Bonus and rights issues

1.3.1 Bonus issues

Bonus issues are free shares given to existing shareholders in proportion to their existing shareholding. For example, a shareholder may own 2,000 shares. The company makes a 1 share for every 2 shares held bonus issue (called a 1 for 2 bonus issue). The shareholder will then have an extra 1,000 shares, giving them 3,000 shares overall.

Bonus shares are treated as being acquired at the date of the original acquisition of the underlying shares giving rise to the bonus issue.

Since bonus shares are issued at no cost there is **no need to adjust the original cost**.

1.3.2 Rights issues

In a **rights issue**, a **shareholder is offered the right to buy additional shares by the company in proportion to the shares already held**.

The difference between a bonus issue and a rights issue is that in a rights issue the new shares are paid for. This results in an **adjustment to the original cost**.

For matching purposes, bonus and rights shares are treated as if they were acquired on the same day as the shareholder's original holdings.

Illustration 4: Bonus and rights issues

Jonah acquired 20,000 shares for £34,200 in T plc in April 2005. There was a 1 for 2 bonus issue in May 2010 and a 1 for 5 rights issue in August 2015 at £1.20 per share.

Jonah sold 30,000 shares for £45,000 in December 2016.

The gain on sale is:

	£
Proceeds of sale	45,000
Less allowable cost (W1)	(34,500)
Chargeable gain	10,500

(W1) The share pool is constructed as follows:

Date	Number of shares	Cost £
April 2005 acquisition	20,000	34,200
May 2010 bonus 1 for 2 (1/2 × 20,000 = 10,000)	10,000	–
	30,000	34,200
August 2015 rights 1 for 5 @ £1.20 (1/5 × 30,000 = 6,000 shares × £1.20 = £7,200)	6,000	7,200
	36,000	41,400
December 2016 disposal (£41,400 × 30,000/36,000 = £34,500)	(30,000)	(34,500)
c/f	6,000	6,900

Activity 3: Bonus and rights issues

Richard had the following transactions in S plc.

1.10.95	Bought 10,000 shares for £15,000
11.9.99	Bought 2,000 shares for £5,000
1.2.00	Took up rights issue 1 for 2 at £2.75 per share
5.9.05	2 for 1 bonus issue
14.10.16	Sold 15,000 shares for £15,000

Required

Calculate the gain or loss made on these shares. All workings must be shown in your calculations.

Solution

	Number	£

Chapter summary

- The matching rules are:

  (1) Same day acquisitions
  (2) Next 30 days' acquisitions on a FIFO basis
  (3) Shares in the share pool

- The share pool runs up to the day before disposal.

- Bonus issue and rights issue shares are acquired in proportion to the shareholder's existing holding.

Keywords

- **Bonus shares:** shares that are issued free to shareholders based on original holdings

- **Rights issues:** similar to bonus issues except that in a rights issue shares must be paid for

Activity answers

Activity 1: Matching rules

	Shares
Same day	400
Next 30 days	500
Share pool	700 ß
Disposal	1,600

(1) Match with same day

	£	£
Proceeds 400/1,600 × 14,000	3,500	
Cost	(3,000)	
		500

(2) Match with next 30 days

	£	£
Proceeds 500/1,600 × 14,000	4,375	
Cost	(4,500)	
		(125)

(3) Match with share pool

	£	£
Proceeds 700/1,600 × 14,000	6,125	
Cost (W)	(2,800)	
		3,325
Net gain		3,700

(W) Share pool

	Number	Cost
15.5.02	2,200	8,800
Disposal 700/2,200 × 8,800	(700)	(2,800)
	1,500	6,000

Activity 2: Share pool

Matching rules: The shares were all acquired prior to the date of disposal so they are all in the share pool.

	£
Proceeds	14,000
Cost (W1)	(4,500)
Gain	9,500

Share pool (W1)

	Number	Cost £
January 1985		
Purchase	3,000	5,000
February 1987		
Purchase	1,000	4,000
	4,000	9,000
May 2016		
Disposal 2,000/4,000 × 9,000	(2,000)	(4,500)
	2,000	4,500

Activity 3: Bonus and rights issues

Matching rules: All bought prior to date of disposal so all from share pool.

Gain

	£
Proceeds	15,000
Less cost (W1)	(10,139)
Gain	4,861

(W1) Share pool

	Number	Cost £
1.10.95	10,000	15,000
11.9.99 acquisition	2,000	5,000
	12,000	20,000
1.2.00 1:2 rights @ £2.75	6,000	16,500
	18,000	36,500
5.9.05 2:1 bonus	36,000	–
	54,000	36,500
14.10.16 sale 15,000/54,000 × 36,500	(15,000)	(10,139)
	39,000	26,361

1 Tasha bought 10,000 shares in V plc in August 1994 for £5,000 and a further 10,000 shares for £16,000 in April 2009. She sold 15,000 shares for £30,000 in November 2016.

Tick to show what her chargeable gain is.

	✓
£15,750	
£11,500	
£17,000	
£14,250	

2 **Tick to show whether the following statement is true or false.**

In both a bonus issue and a rights issue, there is an adjustment to the original cost of the shares.

	✓
True	
False	

3 Marcus bought 2,000 shares in X plc in May 2003 for £12,000. There was a 1 for 2 rights issue at £7.50 per share in December 2004. Marcus sold 2,500 shares for £20,000 in March 2017.

His chargeable gain is:

£

4 Mildred bought 6,000 shares in George plc in June 2011 for £15,000. There was a 1 for 3 bonus issue in August 2012. Mildred sold 8,000 shares for £22,000 in December 2016.

Her chargeable gain is:

£

5 **What are the share matching rules?**

Principal private residence

Learning outcomes

4.7S	Apply reliefs and exemptions

Assessment context

Capital gains tax exemptions will be tested in Task 11 for 6 marks.

Qualification context

You will not be tested on these rules outside of this unit.

Business context

Selling a house could trigger a substantial capital gains tax liability. A practitioner needs to be able to recognise when these rules apply to reduce or exempt the gain.

Chapter overview

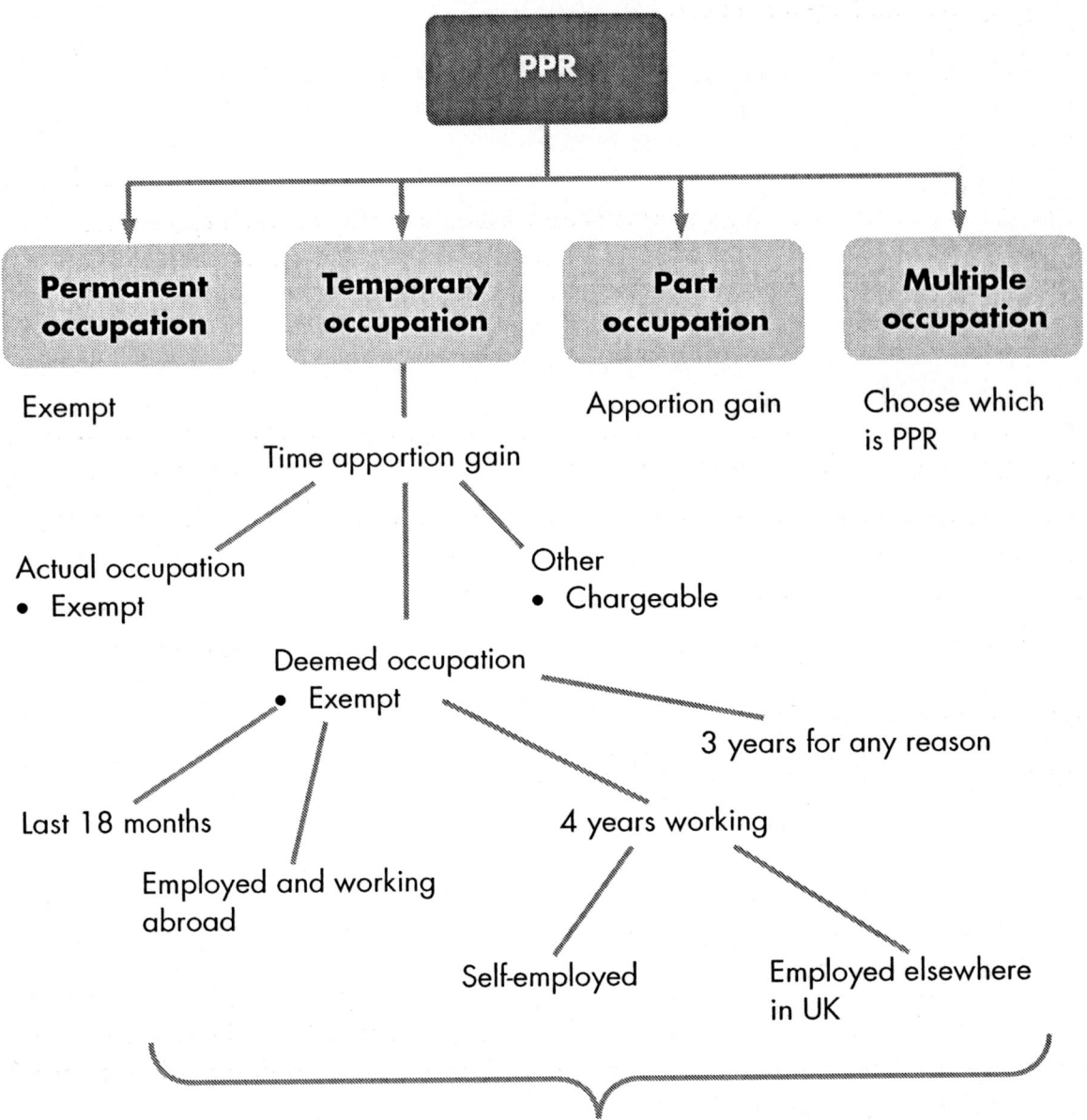

PPR

Permanent occupation

Exempt

Temporary occupation

Time apportion gain

Actual occupation
• Exempt

Other
• Chargeable

Deemed occupation
• Exempt

Last 18 months

Employed and working abroad

3 years for any reason

4 years working

Self-employed

Employed elsewhere in UK

Must have occupied before and after absence

Part occupation

Apportion gain

Multiple occupation

Choose which is PPR

Introduction

In this chapter we're going to look at special rules that apply when a taxpayer sells the property that they have lived in.

1 Principal private residence (PPR) relief

1.1 General rule

Key term

> **Principal private residence** This is an individual's only or main residence. It includes a garden of up to half a hectare.
> There is usually no capital gains tax liability when an individual sells their residence because of PPR relief.

If a taxpayer has lived in the residence **for the whole period of ownership** then there will be **no capital gain when the property is sold**. If the taxpayer has not lived there for the whole period of ownership than **only the gain relating to the period of occupation will be exempt**. This will be calculated by **time apportioning** the gain.

Likewise, if the property is sold at a loss then no capital loss may be claimed.

> **Formula to learn**
>
> **Illustration – PPR relief is calculated as:**
>
> $$\text{Gain} \times \frac{\text{Period of occupation}}{\text{Period of ownership}}$$

1.2 Periods of occupation

Even though the taxpayer may not actually be occupying the property we may be able to treat it for tax purposes as if the taxpayer was actually in residence thus giving exemption from tax. These are what we call periods of **deemed occupation**.

Key term

> **Deemed occupation** A period of time when HMRC will treat the taxpayer as occupying the property for the purposes of claiming PPR relief even though they are not actually there.

The last 18 months are always deemed occupation in full, provided the property was the taxpayer's PPR at some point.

Certain periods of absence are deemed occupation, providing that they are preceded and followed (at any time whatsoever) by actual occupation:

BPP
LEARNING MEDIA

Deemed occupation

- Any period during which the owner was abroad by reason of their employment

- Any periods (not exceeding four years in total) during which the employed owner was required to work away from home in the UK

- Any periods (not exceeding four years in total) during which the owner, if self-employed, was working away from home in the UK or overseas

- Any periods, for whatever reason, not exceeding three years in total

1.3 Part occupation

If any part of the residence is not occupied by the owner for residence purposes, PPR relief will be proportionately withdrawn. For example, if the garage was used as a workshop and one bedroom was used as a home office for a business, then the PPR would only be available on the percentage used for residential purposes.

If the property had been used for different purposes at different times then there would need to be an apportionment of relief based on time and use.

1.4 More than one residence

The taxpayer may choose which home is to be their PPR, provided that each has been occupied at some point.

If the owner is unable to occupy their own home because they are required to occupy job-related accommodation, their own home will be deemed to be their main residence, provided that they intend to occupy it at some point.

1.5 More than one occupier

Married couples/civil partners are only allowed one exemption between them.

Illustration 1: Principal private residence relief

Mr A purchased a house for £50,000 on 31 March 1997. He lived in the house until 30 June 1997. He was then sent to work abroad by his employer for 5 years before returning to the UK to live in the house again on 1 July 2002. He stayed in the house for 6 months before moving out to live with friends until the house was sold on 31 December 2016 for £150,000.

First work out the total period of ownership:

31 March 1997 to 31 December 2016 = 19 years and 9 months (or 237 months).

Next, decide what periods are chargeable and which are exempt:

		Exempt months	Chargeable months
(i)	1 April 1997 to 30 June 1997	3	–
(ii)	1 July 1997 to 30 June 2002	60	–
(iii)	1 July 2002 to 31 December 2002	6	–
(iv)	1 January 2003 to 30 June 2015	–	150
(v)	1 July 2015 to 31 December 2016	18	–
		87	150

Explanations:

(i) **April 1997 to June 1997.** Actual occupation.

(ii) **July 1997 to June 2002.** Covered by the exemption for periods of absence during which the owner is required by his employment to live abroad. The period is both preceded and followed by a period of owner occupation.

(iii) **July 2002 to December 2002.** Actual occupation.

(iv) **January 2003 to June 2015.** This period is not eligible to be partly covered by the exemption for 3 years of absence for any reason, as it is not followed by a period of actual occupation.

(v) **July 2015 to December 2016.** Covered by the final 18 months' exemption.

Then, calculate the chargeable gain after the exemption has been applied:

	£
Disposal proceeds	150,000
Less cost	(50,000)
Gain before PPR	100,000
Less exempt under PPR provisions	
$\dfrac{87}{237} \times £100,000$	(36,709)
Chargeable gain	63,291

In this example, had Mr A gone straight to live with friends in July 2001 instead of having six months' occupation, he would have lost not only the extra six months but also the period from July 1997 to June 2002. This period of absence would lose its status of deemed occupation as the property would not have been occupied again by the owner prior to sale.

Activity 1: Principal private residence relief

Harry bought his house in London on 1 April 1990 and lived in it until 1 April 1991. From that date until 1 April 1993, he was required by his employers to work overseas.

He returned to the UK on 1 April 1993 to work for his employers in Bristol but lived in rented accommodation there as it was too far to travel daily from London to Bristol to work. He returned to the house on 1 April 1996 for six months. From then on, he moved out to go and live with his mother where he remained until he sold his house on 30 September 2016, realising a gain of £100,000.

Required

Complete the following sentence:

The gain on the disposal of his house is £ [   ]

Chapter summary

- Any gain arising on the disposal of an individual's principal private residence is exempt from CGT if the individual has occupied/deemed to have occupied the property throughout the period of ownership. A loss on disposal is not allowable.

- If there have been periods of non-occupation, then part of any gain on disposal may be chargeable.

- Certain periods of non-occupation count as periods of deemed occupation.

- The last 18 months of ownership always count as a period of occupation if, at some time, the residence has been the taxpayer's main residence.

Keywords

- **Deemed occupation:** periods during which an individual is treated as having occupied a residence

- **Principal private residence:** an individual's only or main residence

Activity answers

Activity 1: Principal private residence relief

The gain on the disposal of his house is £ | 69,811 |

Workings

PPR – periods of absence	Occ. (mths)	Non-Occ. (mths)	
1.4.90–31.3.91			
(occupation)	12		
1.4.91–31.3.93			
(working overseas)	24		
1.4.93–31.3.96			
(up to 4 years working in UK)	36		
1.4.96–30.9.96			
(occupation)	6		
1.10.96–31.3.15			
(no deemed occupation as property not reoccupied)		222	
1.4.15–30.9.16			
(Last 18 months)	18		
	96	222	= 318

Capital gain	£
Gain	100,000
Less PPR	
$100,000 \times \dfrac{96}{318}$	(30,189)
Gain	69,811

1   Provided the property has at some time been the owner's principal private residence, the last .... months of ownership is always an exempt period.

Tick ONE box.

	✓
12	
18	
24	
36	

2   **Explain three examples of periods of absence from a property which are deemed periods of occupation for the CGT principal private residence exemption.**

3   Josephine purchased a house on 1 April 1999 for £60,000 and used it as her main residence until 1 August 2002 when she was sent by her employer to manage the Paris office. She worked and lived in Paris until 31 July 2006. Josephine returned to live in the house on 1 August 2006 but moved out to live in a new house (to be treated as her main residence) on 1 May 2008. The property was empty until sold on 30 November 2016 for £180,000.

Using the proforma below, compute the gain on sale.

	£
Proceeds	
Cost	
Gain before PPR exemption	
PPR exemption	
Chargeable gain	

4   Noddy is selling his main residence, which he has owned for 25 years. He lived in the house for the first 14 years of ownership then, for the next 5 years, he was posted abroad by his employer. He never returned to live in the house during the remainder of his period of ownership.

What fraction of his gain will be exempt under the private residence exemption?

Tick ONE box.

	✓
20.5/25	
14/25	
15.5/25	
19/25	

5   Clare bought herself a flat in April 2011 for £80,000. She lived in the flat until December 2015 when she moved to a farmhouse she had bought to be her main residence. The flat was empty until it was sold in March 2017 for £300,000.

Decide whether the following statement is true or false.

Tick ONE box.

The gain arising on the sale is completely exempt.

	✓
True	
False	

Test your learning: answers

Chapter 1 The tax framework

1

Statement	True ✓	False ✓
All taxpayers are sent a tax return each year by HM Revenue & Customs.		✓

Most taxpayers are employees who have their tax deducted at source under PAYE so they do not need to complete a tax return.

2

	✓
The Chancellor of the Exchequer	
Companies House	
HM Revenue & Customs	✓
Members of Parliament	

3

	✓
Acts of Parliament	✓
HMRC statements of practice	
Statutory instruments	✓
Extra statutory concessions	

4

	✓
When in a social environment	
When discussing client affairs with third parties with the client's proper and specific authority	✓
When reading documents relating to the a client's affairs in public places	
When preparing tax returns	

5

	✓
HMRC	
Nearest police station	
National Crime Agency	✓
Tax tribunal	

6   You should tell Cornelius that under the AAT guidelines on client confidentiality, you cannot provide him with any information on another client without the specific authority of that client.

Chapter 2 Payment of tax and tax administration

1   The due filing date for an income tax return for 2016/17 assuming the taxpayer will submit the return online is

> 31/01/2018

2   The 2017/18 payments on account will be calculated as

> 50%

of the income tax payable for

> 2016/17

and will be due on

> 31 January 2018

and

> 31 July 2018

3   £100 penalty for failure to deliver return on time.

Possible £10 per day penalty from 1 May 2018 until date of filing.

5% penalty on tax paid late. Interest on tax paid late.

4

	✓
31 January 2019	
31 March 2019	
6 April 2019	
28 January 2019	✓

5 Jamie's 2016/17 payments on account will each be

£6,000

and will be due on

31/01/2017

and

31/07/2017

Jamie's balancing payment will be

£4,000

and will be due on

31/01/2018

6 £ | 0 |

No penalties for late payment are due on late payments on account.

7 (a)

	✓
30 September 2017	
31 October 2017	✓
31 December 2017	
31 January 2018	

Paper returns must usually be submitted by 31 October following the end of the tax year.

(b)

	✓
31 January 2018 and 31 July 2018	
31 January 2017 and 31 July 2017	✓
31 October 2017 and 31 January 2018	
31 July 2017 and 31 January 2018	

Payments on account are due on 31 January in the tax year and 31 July following the end of the tax year.

8

	✓
£5,100	
£3,400	
£1,020	✓
£2,380	

$30\% \times PLR =$ **£1,020**

$PLR = £17,000 \times 20\% = £3,400$

Chapter 3 Employment income

1   Someone is regarded as self-employed if they have a contract ⌈ for services ⌉ , whereas if they have a contract ⌈ of service ⌉ , they will be regarded as an employee.

2   Expenses are deductible in computing taxable earnings if they are incurred ⌈ wholly ⌉ , ⌈ exclusively ⌉ and ⌈ necessarily ⌉ in the performance of the duties of employment.

3   The amounts that are taxable/(deductible) in calculating employment income are £ ⌈ (800) ⌉

Working

	£
Amount received: 8,000 × 35p	2,800
Less statutory limit: 8,000 × 45p	(3,600)
Deductible amount	(800)

4   £ ⌈ 5,900 ⌉

being the higher of the annual value and rent actually paid by the employer.

5

	✓
True	
False	✓

There is a taxable fuel benefit unless the employer is fully reimbursed for private fuel.

6

	✓
£325	
£400	
£175	
£250	✓

Working

The benefit is the higher of:

		£	£
(a)	Current MV	325	
(b)	Original MV	500	
	Less already assessed (in 2016/17)		
	£500 × 20%	(100)	
		400	
			400
	Less amount paid		(150)
	Taxable benefit		250

7

	✓
True	
False	✓

Only if total loans do not exceed £10,000 at any time in the tax year are they ignored.

8   £ [6,480]

Working

CO₂ emissions = 150 g/km (rounded down)
Above baseline: $150 - 95$ = 55 g/km
Divide by 5 = 55/5 = 11
Percentage = 16% + 11% = 27%
Benefit 27% × £24,000 = £6,480

9 £ 28,260

	£
Car benefit (W)	21,600
Fuel benefit (£22,200 × 30%)	6,660
Telephone benefit (exempt – one mobile phone)	Nil
Total benefit	28,260

Working

Amount of emissions above baseline: 165 – 95 = 70 g/km
Divide 70 by 5 = 14
Percentage = 16% + 14% = 30%
£72,000 × 30% = £21,600

10

Item	Taxable	Exempt
Write off loan of £8,000 (only loan provided)	✓	☐
Payments by employer of £500 per month into registered pension scheme	☐	✓
Provision of one mobile phone	☐	✓
Provision of a company car for both business and private use	✓	☐
Removal costs of £5,000 paid to an employee relocating to another branch	☐	✓
Accommodation provided to enable the employee to spend longer time in the office	✓	☐

Chapter 4 Property income

1 £ 1,200

Rent accrued 1 December 2016 to 5 April 2017 = 4/12 × £3,600

2 £ 5,000

Working

Insurance premiums accrued in 2016/17:

	£
6/12 × £4,800 (6 April 2016 to 30 September 2016)	2,400
6/12 × £5,200 (1 October 2016 to 5 April 2017)	2,600
	5,000

3   Losses from furnished holiday lettings can only be carried forward against future profits from the same furnished holiday lettings business.

4   The income qualifies as earnings for pension purposes. Primarily this gives scope for relief for higher pension contributions.

5   £ [1,667]

Working

	£
Rental income (£4,000 × 8/12)	2,667
Less expenses	(1,000)
Taxable rental income	1,667

Rent of £5,000, paid on 4 April 2017 accrues in 2017/18 and is therefore taxed in that year.

6

	✓
£3,750	
£4,250	
£7,500	✓
£10,000	

7

	✓
Income can qualify as 'earnings' for pension purposes	
Capital allowances can be claimed on furniture	
Replacement relief can be claimed on furniture	✓
Losses can be set against other income – not just property income	✓

Chapter 5 Taxable income

1

	Non-savings income	Savings income	Dividend income
Employment income	☑	☐	☐
Dividends	☐	☐	☑
Property income	☑	☐	☐
Bank interest	☐	☑	☐
Pension income	☑	☐	☐
Interest on government stock	☐	☑	☐

2

	Amount received £	Amount in tax return £
Building society interest	240	240
Interest on an individual savings account	40	0
Dividends	160	160
Interest from government gilts	350	350

3

	Non-savings income £	Dividend income £	Total £
Employment income	30,000		30,000
Dividends		300	300
Net income	30,000	300	30,300
Less personal allowance	(11,000)		(11,000)
Taxable income	19,000	300	19,300

Premium bond winnings are exempt from income tax.

4

	Non-savings income £	Savings income £	Total £
Property income	3,000		3,000
Building society interest		9,000	9,000
Net income	3,000	9,000	12,000
Less personal allowance	(3,000)	(8,000)	(11,000)
Taxable income	Nil	1,000	1,000

The personal allowance is deducted first from non-savings income and then from savings income.

5

	Non-savings income £	Savings income £	Dividend income £	Total £
Employment income	112,200			112,200
Building society interest		5,000		5,000
Dividends			4,000	4,000
Net income	112,200	5,000	4,000	121,200
Less personal allowance (W)	(400)			(400)
Taxable income	111,800	5,000	4,000	120,800

Working

	£
Net income	121,200
Less income limit	(100,000)
Excess	21,200
Personal allowance	11,000
Less half excess	(10,600)
Adjusted personal allowance	400

The prize is exempt from income tax.

Chapter 6 Calculation of income tax

1

	✓
0%, 20%, 40% and 45%	
40% and 45%	
20% only	
20%, 40% and 45%	✓

2 £ 1,320

Working

	Non-savings income £	Savings income £	Dividend income £	Total £
Net income	16,600	2,000	3,000	21,600
Less personal allowance	(11,000)	–	–	(11,000)
Taxable income	5,600	2,000	3,000	10,600

	£
Tax on non-savings income	
5,600 × 20%	1,120
Tax on savings income	
1,000 × 0%	0
1,000 × 20%	200
Tax on dividend income	
3,000 × 0%	0
Tax liability	1,320

Albert is a basic rate taxpayer so has a personal savings allowance of £1,000. The dividend allowance is always £5,000.

3   £ [3,075]

Working

	Non-savings income £	Savings income £	Dividend income £	Total £
Employment income	5,000			5,000
Interest		18,000		18,000
Dividends			22,000	22,000
Net income	5,000	18,000	22,000	45,000
Less personal allowance	(5,000)	(6,000)		11,000
Taxable income	Nil	12,000	22,000	34,000

	£
Tax on savings income	
5,000 × 0%	0
500 × 0%	0
6,500 × 20%	1,300
12,000	
Tax on dividend income	
5,000 × 0%	0
15,000 × 7.5%	1,125
32,000	
2,000 × 32.5%	650
34,000	
Income tax liability	3,075

Net income is > £43,000 < £151,000 so personal savings allowance of £500 available. Dividend allowance of £5,000 always available.

4 £ ┌─────────┐
         │ 67,625 │
         └─────────┘

Working

	Non-savings income £	Savings income £	Dividend income £	Total £
Employment income	140,000			140,000
Interest		20,000		20,000
Dividends			30,000	30,000
Net income	140,000	20,000	30,000	190,000
Less personal allowance	(Nil)			(Nil)
Taxable income	140,000	20,000	30,000	190,000

The personal allowance and personal savings allowance are nil because the net income is so high.

	£
Tax on non-savings income	
32,000 × 20%	6,400
108,000 × 40%	43,200
140,000	
Tax on savings income	
10,000 × 40%	4,000
150,000	
10,000 × 45%	4,500
160,000	
Tax on dividend income	
5,000 × 0%	0
25,000 × 38.1%	9,525
190,000	
Income tax liability	67,625

5   Basic rate tax relief is obtained by paying Gift Aid donations net of 20% tax. Further tax relief is given to higher and additional rate taxpayers by extending the basic and higher rate bands by the gross amount of the Gift Aid donation.

6

	Non-savings income £	Savings income £	Dividend income £	Total £
Pension income	17,000			17,000
Property income	3,500			3,500
Interest (received gross)		380		380
Dividends			700	700
Net income	20,500	380	700	21,580
Less personal allowance	(11,000)			(11,000)
Taxable income	9,500	380	700	10,580

Premium bond prizes are exempt from income tax. She is a basic rate taxpayer so receives the full personal savings allowance of £1,000. The £5,000 dividend allowance is also available.

	£
Tax on non-savings income	
£9,500 × 20%	1,900
Tax on savings income	
£380 × 0%	0
Tax on dividend income	
£700 × 0%	0
	1,900
Less tax deducted from pension income (given)	(2,010)
Income tax repayable	(110)

7

	Non-savings income £	Savings income £	Dividend income £	Total £
Business profits	36,600			36,600
Building society interest		2,000		2,000
Dividends			8,000	8,000
Net income	36,600	2,000	8,000	46,600
Less personal allowance	(11,000)			(11,000)
Taxable income	25,600	2,000	8,000	35,600

	£
Tax on non-savings income	
£25,600 × 20%	5,120
Tax on savings income	
£500 × 0%	0
£1,500 × 20%	300
Tax on dividend income	
£5,000 × 0%	0
£1,400 × 7.5% £34,000	105
£1,600 × 32.5% (£8,000 – £5,000 – £1,400)	520
Income tax liability/payable	6,045

Note. Gross Gift Aid payment = £1,600 × 100/80 = £2,000. Basic rate extends to £34,000.

Adjusted net income = £46,600 – £2,000 = £44,600 > £43,000 so £500 personal savings allowance available

8

	✓
£32,000	
£47,000	
£50,750	✓
£57,000	

Working

£15,000 × 100/80 = £18,750 + £32,000

Chapter 7 Chargeable gains

1

	Chargeable ✓	Exempt ✓
A gift of an antique necklace	✓	
The sale of a building	✓	
Sale of a racehorse		✓

2

	£
Proceeds of sale	200,000
Less cost	(80,000)
Less enhancement expenditure	(10,000)
Chargeable gain	110,000

3 £ 144,600

   £ 0

	£
Gains	171,000
Less current year losses	(5,300)
	165,700
Less losses b/f	(10,000)
	155,700
Less annual exempt amount	(11,100)
Taxable gains	144,600

4 £ ☐ 2,560 ☐

	£
Chargeable gains	23,900
Less annual exempt amount	(11,100)
Taxable gains	12,800
CGT on £12,800 @ 20%	2,560

5 ☐ 31/01/2018 ☐

6

	✓
£16,663	✓
£17,500	
£19,663	
£18,337	

	£
Proceeds	38,000
Less costs of disposal	(3,000)
	35,000
Less £41,500 × $\dfrac{38,000}{38,000+48,000}$	(18,337)
Chargeable gain	16,663

7 (a)

£	Nil

There is no gain as the chattel cost and gross proceeds are both less than £6,000.

(b)

£	4,033

	£
Gross proceeds	8,420
Less selling expenses	(220)
Net proceeds	8,200
Less cost	(3,500)
	4,700

Gain cannot exceed 5/3 (8,420 – 6,000) = £4,033

Therefore, gain is £4,033

8

	✓
True	
False	✓

A loss on a disposal to a connected person can be set only against gains arising on disposals to the same connected person.

9

	✓
True	✓
False	

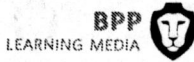

	Actual proceeds used	Deemed proceeds (market value) used	No gain or loss basis
Paul sells an asset to his civil partner Joe for £3,600.			✓
Grandmother gives an asset to her grandchild worth £1,000.		✓	
Sarah sells an asset worth £20,000 to her best friend Cathy for £12,000. Sarah knows the asset is worth £20,000.		✓	

Chapter 8 Share disposals

1

	✓
£15,750	
£11,500	
£17,000	
£14,250	✓

	No of shares	Cost £
August 1994 acquisition	10,000	5,000
April 2009 acquisition	10,000	16,000
	20,000	21,000
November 2016 disposal	(15,000)	(15,750)
(£21,000 × 15,000/20,000 = £15,750)		
c/f	5,000	5,250

	No of shares	Cost £
Proceeds of sale		30,000
Less allowable cost		(15,750)
Chargeable gain		14,250

2

	✓
True	
False	✓

In a rights issue, shares are paid for and this amount is added to the original cost. In a bonus issue, shares are not paid for and so there is no adjustment to the original cost.

3 £ | 3,750 |

	No of shares	Cost £
May 2003 acquisition	2,000	12,000
December 2004 1 for 2 rights issue @ £7.50	1,000	7,500
(1/2 × 2,000 = 1,000 shares × £7.50 = £7,500)		
	3,000	19,500
March 2017 disposal	(2,500)	(16,250)
(£19,500 × 2,500/3,000)		
c/f	500	3,250

	£
Proceeds of sale	20,000
Less allowable costs	(16,250)
Chargeable gain	3,750

4   £ | 7,000 |

	No of shares	Cost £
June 2011 acquisition	6,000	15,000
August 2012 1 for 3 bonus issue (1/3 × 6,000 = 2,000 shares)	2,000	nil
	8,000	15,000
December 2016 disposal (ie all the shares)	(8,000)	(15,000)
c/f	nil	nil

	£
Proceeds of sale	22,000
Less allowable costs	(15,000)
Chargeable gain	7,000

5   The matching rules for shares disposed of are:

    (a)   Shares acquired on the same day

    (b)   Shares acquired in the next 30 days

    (c)   Shares from the share pool

Chapter 9 Principal private residence

1

	✓
12	
18	✓
24	
36	

2   The last 18 months of ownership is deemed occupation if, at some time, the residence has been the taxpayer's main residence.

Providing the taxpayer actually occupies the property both at some point before and at some point after the period of absence, the following periods are deemed occupation for the purpose of PPR exemption:

(a) Periods of up to three years for any reason. Where a period of absence exceeds three years, three years out of the longer period are deemed to be a period of occupation.

(b) Periods during which the owner was required by their employment to live abroad.

(c) Period of up to four years where the owner was:

    (i) Self-employed and forced to work away from home (UK and abroad)

    (ii) Employed and required to work elsewhere in the UK (overseas employment is covered by (b) above)

3

	£
Proceeds	180,000
Cost	(60,000)
Gain before PPR exemption	120,000
PPR exemption 127/212 × £120,000	(71,887)
Chargeable gain	48,113

Working

Total period of ownership: 1 April 1999 to 30 November 2016 = 17 years and 8 months (212 months)

Item	Exempt months	Chargeable months
1 April 1999 to 31 July 2002 (actual occupation)	40	
1 August 2002 to 31 July 2006 (employed abroad)	48	
1 August 2006 to 30 April 2008 (actual occupation)	21	
1 May 2008 to 31 May 2015		85
1 June 2015 to 30 November 2016		
(last 18 months)	18	
	127	85

Exempt 127/212 × £120,000 = £71,887

4

	✓
20.5/25	
14/25	
15.5/25	✓
19/25	

The five years posted abroad will not be deemed occupation as he never returned to live in the property. Therefore, only the actual 14 years of occupation and the last 18 months of ownership will be exempt.

5

	✓
True	✓
False	

Clare was in actual occupation from April 2011 to December 2015.

The last 18 months of ownership are exempt because Clare had previously lived in the flat as her only or main residence. Therefore, this covers her period of absence from December 2015 to March 2017.

Taxation tables for personal tax – 2016/17

Tax rates and bands

	%	£
Basic rate	20	first 32,000
Higher rate	40	to 150,000
Additional rate	45	over 150,000

Dividends are taxed at 7.5%, 32.5% and 38.1%.

Personal allowances

	£
Personal allowance for individuals	11,000
Savings allowance – basic rate taxpayers	1,000
Higher rate taxpayer	500
Dividend allowance	5,000
Income limit for personal allowances	100,000

Individual savings accounts

	£
Annual limit	15,240

Car benefit percentage

Emission rating for petrol engines	%
0 g/km to 50 g/km	7
51 g/km to 75 g/km	11
76 g/km to 94 g/km	15
95 g/km or more	16 + 1% for every extra 5 g/km above 95 g/km

Diesel engines – additional 3%
Electric vehicles – 7%

The figure for fuel is £22,200.

Approved mileage allowance payments

First 10,000 miles	45p
Over 10,000 miles	25p

Van scale charge

Charge	£3,170
Private fuel provided	£598
Benefit charge for zero emission vans	20%

HMRC official rate	3%
Capital gains tax	
Annual exemption	£11,100
Tax rate	10%
Higher rate	20%

Bibliography

Association of Accounting Technicians (2014) *AAT Code of Professional Ethics. Version 2.* [eBook] London, AAT. Available from: www.aat.org.uk/sites/default/files/assets/AAT_Code_of_Professional_Ethics.pdf [Accessed on 14 July 2016].

Association of Accounting Technicians (2016) *Personal Tax (Level 4) Study and assessment guide Version: Finance Act 2015.* [Online] Available from: www.aat.org.uk/system/files/study_resources/L4-personal-tax-study-and-assessment-guide-FA2015.pdf [Accessed on 14 July 2016].

Association of Accounting Technicians (2016) *Sample Assessment AQ2013 PTAX FA15.* [Online] Available from: www.aat-interactive.org.uk/elearning/Sample_assessments_AQ2013/ AQ2013_PTAX_FA15_sample1/index.html [Accessed on 14 July 2016].

Her Majesty's Revenue and Customs (2014) *Expenses & benefits: A tax guide.* [Online] Available from: www.gov.uk/government/uploads/system/uploads/attachment_data/file/314687 /480-2014.pdf [Accessed on 16th August 2016].

Her Majesty's Revenue and Customs (2016) *Self-Assessment Tax Return Form Employment Income Page (SA102).* [Online] Available from: www.gov.uk/government/uploads/system/uploads/attachment_data/file/501125 /sa102-2016.pdf [Accessed on 14 July 2016].

Her Majesty's Revenue and Customs (2016) *Self-Assessment Tax Return Form UK Property Income Page (SA105).* [Online] Available from: www.gov.uk/government/uploads/system/uploads/attachment_data/file/501201 /sa105-2016.pdf [Accessed on 14 July 2016].

Her Majesty's Revenue and Customs (2016) *Self-Assessment Tax Return Form Capital Gains Summary Page (SA108).* [Online] Available from: www.gov.uk/government/uploads/system/uploads/attachment_data/file/501338 /sa108-2016.pdf [Accessed on 14 July 2016].

Contains public sector information licensed under the Open Government Licence v3.0. www.nationalarchives.gov.uk/doc/open-government-licence/version/3/.

REVIEW FORM

How have you used this Course Book?
(Tick one box only)

☐ Self study

☐ On a course_____

☐ Other _____

Why did you decide to purchase this Course Book? *(Tick one box only)*

☐ Have used BPP materials in the past

☐ Recommendation by friend/colleague

☐ Recommendation by a college lecturer

☐ Saw advertising

☐ Other _____

During the past six months do you recall seeing/receiving either of the following?
(Tick as many boxes as are relevant)

☐ Our advertisement in Accounting Technician

☐ Our Publishing Catalogue

Which (if any) aspects of our advertising do you think are useful?
(Tick as many boxes as are relevant)

☐ Prices and publication dates of new editions

☐ Information on Course Book content

☐ Details of our free online offering

☐ None of the above

Your ratings, comments and suggestions would be appreciated on the following areas of this Course Book.

	Very useful	Useful	Not useful
Chapter overviews	☐	☐	☐
Introductory section	☐	☐	☐
Quality of explanations	☐	☐	☐
Illustrations	☐	☐	☐
Chapter activities	☐	☐	☐
Test your learning	☐	☐	☐
Keywords	☐	☐	☐

	Excellent	Good	Adequate	Poor
Overall opinion of this Course Book	☐	☐	☐	☐

Do you intend to continue using BPP Products? ☐ Yes ☐ No

Please note any further comments and suggestions/errors on the reverse of this page and return it to: Nisar Ahmed, AAT Head of Programme, BPP Learning Media Ltd, FREEPOST, London, W12 8AA.

Alternatively, the Head of Programme of this edition can be emailed at: nisarahmed@bpp.com

REVIEW FORM (continued)

TELL US WHAT YOU THINK

Please note any further comments and suggestions/errors below